Specter's

What Not to Do

HAWAII

A Unique Travel Guide

Plan your travel with expert advice and Insider Tips: Travel confidently, Avoid Common Mistakes, and indulge in Art, Culture, History, Food, and nature.

Sarah Brekenridge

Specter Publication

What NOT To Do - Hawaii

© Copyright 2024 – Specter Publication LLC.

The content contained within this book may not be reproduced, duplicated, or transmitted without direct written permission from the author or the publisher.

Under no circumstances will any blame or legal responsibility be held against the publisher, or author, for any damages, reparation, or monetary loss due to the information contained within this book, either directly or indirectly.

Legal Notice:

This book is copyright-protected. It is only for personal use. You cannot amend, distribute, sell, use, quote, or paraphrase any part, or the content within this book, without the consent of the author or publisher.

Disclaimer Notice:

Please note the information contained within this document is for educational and entertainment purposes only. All effort has been executed to present accurate, up-to-date, reliable, and complete information. No warranties of any kind are declared or implied. Readers acknowledge that the author is not engaged in the rendering of legal, financial, medical, or professional advice. The content within this book has been derived from various sources. Please consult a licensed professional before attempting any techniques outlined in this book.

By reading this document, the reader agrees that under no circumstances is the author responsible for any direct or indirect losses incurred as a result of the use of the information contained within this document, including, but not limited to, errors, omissions, or inaccuracies.

Table of Contents

Introduction...8

Chapter 1: Planning Your Hawaiian Adventure 10

Uncovering Hawaii...10

Peak Hawaii Travel Times.. 13

Flying to Hawaii – Dos and Don'ts.........................14

Hawaii Packing Essentials..16

Hawaii Travel – Dos and Don'ts..............................18

Chapter 2: Tips and Tricks to Explore Hawaii.............21

How to Get around Hawaii..................................... 21

Staying Safe in Hawaii.. 22

Dos and Don'ts of Respecting Hawaiian Culture............... 24

Chapter 3: Hawaii Island – Dos and Don'ts 28

Discovering the Island of Hawaii.............................. 28

What to Do on the Island of Hawaii.................................. 29

The Island of Hawaii Beaches 35

What Events to Enjoy on the Island of Hawaii.................. 38

Where to Eat on the Island of Hawaii 40

What to Eat on the Island of Hawaii 43

Where to Stay on the Island of Hawaii 45

What NOT to Do on the Island of Hawaii 47

Chapter 4: Maui Island – Dos and Don'ts 50

Discovering the Island of Maui 50

What to Do on the Island of Maui 51

The Island of Maui Beaches 60

What Events to Enjoy on the Island of Maui 61

Where to Eat on the Island of Maui 62

What to Eat on the Island of Maui 66

Where to Stay on the Island of Maui 67

What NOT to Do on the Island of Maui 70

Chapter 5: Molokai Island – Dos and Don'ts 72

Discovering the Island of Molokai 72

What to Do on the Island of Molokai 73

The Island of Molokai Beaches 76

Where to Eat on the Island of Molokai 78

What to Eat on the Island of Molokai 81

Where to Stay on the Island of Molokai 82

What NOT to Do on the Island of Molokai 83

Chapter 6: Oahu Islands – Dos and Don'ts 85

Discovering the Island of Oahu 85

What to Do on the Island of Oahu 86

The Island of Oahu Beaches 94

What Events to Enjoy on the Island of Oahu 96

Where to Eat on the Island of Oahu 97

What to Eat on the Island of Oahu 100

Where to Stay on the Island of Oahu 101

What NOT to Do on the Island of Oahu 103

Chapter 7: Kauai Island – Dos and Don'ts....................105

Discovering the Island of Kauai... 105

What to Do on the Island of Kauai... 106

The Island of Kauai Beaches 112

What Events to Enjoy on the Island of Kauai 115

Where to Eat on the Island of Kauai 116

What to Eat on the Island of Kauai 119

Where to Stay on the Island of Kauai 120

What NOT to Do on the Island of Kauai 123

Conclusion... 124

References.. 125

Introduction

When you step off the plane in Hawaii, you feel a different vibe. It's paradise infused with something more, known as the "Aloha Spirit."

Aloha is more than a greeting or a farewell used among the Hawaiians—it captures the spirit of life within its beautiful waters and stunning landscapes. Each of its islands holds a treasure, and the Aloha Spirit inspires you to connect with its nature and beauty.

Where do you begin planning a trip to a fantastic state that calls to adventure seekers and romantics alike? Journeying here is a dream for many, but the reality of planning your vacation can quickly become overwhelming. There is so much information on what attractions you should see that worrying about how you'll get from point A to point B can feel daunting. But that's where I come in to help you navigate your way so you can make your Hawaiian vacation dreams a reality.

With so much to see and do, how do you choose your top priorities? In this book, we'll go through the highlights of each Hawaiian island, helping you decide what your must-visit destinations within each should be. You'll be able to streamline the planning process of your trip, saving you time and stress. Whether or not you've been to Hawaii, this book will provide a comprehensive list of suggestions and budgeting tips to ensure you can make the most of your time in paradise.

Once you know what you want to see and do, you may wonder how to get there. Hawaii has plenty of transportation options to allow you to move around its different islands. But have no fear—it's not as complex as you might think, so you can focus on soaking up the beauty around you.

While Hawaii mostly has a mild climate, Mother Nature can throw a curveball occasionally. That shouldn't dampen your trip, though. We'll also explore some safety tips and emergency preparedness to ensure you feel confident navigating any potential weather-related challenges for peace of mind.

What you can expect from reading *What Not to Do When in Hawaii* is a trip companion highlighting the local Hawaiian experience while avoiding some of the more expensive or generic tourist traps, restaurants, and accommodations. From this book, you will discover everything you need to know for your trip to Hawaii, getting in-depth travel guides for Hawaii's islands. This will help you create your dream Hawaiian vacation around an itinerary that will work for you.

I have a wealth of travel experience, so let me guide you whether you are embarking on a solo adventure, a romantic getaway, or a family vacation. This is the start of planning your dream vacation, but the memories you will make will last a lifetime. Let's get started!

Chapter 1:

Planning Your Hawaiian Adventure

D id you know the name Hawaii translates to the "land of the deities"? Back before Hawaii became the famous state it is today, Hawaii had a fascinating origin that stems from the Proto-Polynesian word Hawaiki, which reflects the rich heritage of Hawaii and their ancestors, Māori, who came to the island from New Zealand, navigating the ocean in their canoes.

Hawaiki reflects life in Hawaii, from when humans are born to when they rest for the final time. It is also a word that represents the good and powerful, but also has mythical ideals attached to it where humans shape-shift into birds and go to the underworld.

Hawaii is more than a paradise. It is a place steeped in history and mythology and known for its unique way of life.

Uncovering Hawaii

History of Hawaii

When most people think of Hawaii, they think of the lei gifted to you when you step off the plane, hula dancing, and luau parties. However, this state has years of rich

What NOT To Do - Hawaii

history that few think about when they first consider traveling to Hawaii. Most interestingly, Polynesian settlers migrated to these islands around 300 years ago and established the Hawaiian society, bringing their language, customs, and agricultural techniques with them. Centuries later, King Kamehameha I unified the Hawaiian Islands into a single kingdom. However, this unity was disrupted when British Explorer Captain James Cook arrived at Waimea, Kauai Island, in 1778, foreshadowing significant changes to Hawaiian society with new connections to the West.

The 19th century saw further changes to Hawaiian culture, with the overthrowing of Queen Liliuokalani in 1893, leading to Hawaii's annexation by the US under President William McKinley. In 1959, Hawaii officially became the 50th state of the United States and has seen a rapid change in the population and economy ever since, complete with tourism. However, many of the locals and their earlier generations still work to maintain Hawaii's culture, language, and traditions to foster a renewed sense of pride and connection among those who live in Hawaii.

Hawaii's Landscape

Hawaii has a stunning landscape that might be the most unique of any other place on Earth. Hawaii's beaches are renowned for their pristine beauty and turquoise waters stretching for miles along the coastline. These beaches are perfect for soaking up the Hawaiian sun and enjoying outdoor activities, including surfing and snorkeling.

Underwater volcanoes first formed the Hawaiian Islands. However, Big Island is the only island still with active volcanoes because it is positioned near the hot spot in the Pacific Ocean. Visitors can explore these volcanoes (when it is safe to do so) and witness the raw power of nature as molten lava flows from the Earth's crust, creating new land formations and continually evolving Big Island's terrain over time.

Beyond the beaches and volcanoes, Hawaii's landscapes are diverse, ranging from dense rainforests in Hawaii's lowlands with thousands of flora and fauna species to rugged mountain ranges with stunning waterfalls. Because the islands have many microclimates, each region has a unique ecosystem and scenery to explore.

Moreover, Hawaii's geography and landscape are shaped by its remote location, with the Pacific Ocean surrounding its main and smaller islands. This creates a rich marine environment bursting with biodiversity. If you snorkel, you'll explore the colorful coral reefs, thousands of fish, and much more!

Hawaii's Language and Culture

Hawaiians have worked hard to preserve their language and culture as it is deeply rooted in Hawaii's diverse heritage and history. The Hawaiian language, known as 'Ōlelo Hawai'i, is a Polynesian language connected to the islands' ancient traditions. This language is widely spoken and accepted next to English. Its rhythmic cadence and melodic sounds characterize it, reflecting the Hawaiian people's relationship to the island's nature.

Hawaiian culture is based on several values, including aloha (love, affection, and compassion), kuleana (responsibility), and pono (righteousness). These values are expressed through various aspects of Hawaiian life, including the traditional dance of hula, mele (music and songs), and the oral traditions and storytelling of mo'olelo.

Of course, one of the most iconic symbols of Hawaiian culture is the lei, a garland made with flowers, leaves, shells, feathers, or other materials that are gifted as a symbol of friendship, love, honor, or celebration. They are also used in the essence of aloha and given to visitors coming to Hawaii. Interestingly, this tradition dates back to when the Polynesian voyagers arrived in the Hawaiian Islands after a long journey from Tahiti.

Hawaii's Celebrated Cuisine

In addition to its customs and culture that make Hawaii a beautiful place to see and experience, you'll find that Hawaii is home to a diverse mix of cultures and ethnicities, including Japanese, Chinese, Filipino, and Portuguese—all of which add their influence to Hawaii's cuisine. While the iconic dish in Hawaii is poke, made with raw fish seasoned with soy sauce, sesame oil, and other flavorful ingredients, you'll find Chinese-inspired dim sum and Filipino adobo on restaurant menus. You'll also find plenty of fresh fruit that you can enjoy or has been incorporated into desserts and beverages. However, shaved ice is a must-try if you want a refreshing treat. This delicious, sweet treat is made with finely shaved ice topped with flavored syrups, condensed milk, and fresh fruit.

Hawaii's Celebrated Cities and Landmarks

While Hawaii has plenty of small islands and inlets to explore, it also has celebrated cities and landmarks that attract visitors from afar. Honolulu is the capital city on the island of Oahu. It bursts with vibrant energy and is well-known for its iconic Waikiki Beach, Iolani Palace, and the USS Arizona memorial (also known as Pearl Harbor).

On the Big Island, you can explore the town of Hilo, known for its rainforests, stunning waterfalls, and the famous Hilo farmer's market. Of course, if you go here, you'll also want to explore the volcanoes!

The island of Maui, also known as the "Valley Isle," boasts beautiful beaches, including the famous Kā'anapali Beach. The charming town of Lahaina offers historical sites to explore, art galleries, and beautiful waterfront dining options. If you venture to Halekalā National Park, you can take in stunning views from the summit of the dormant Halekalā Volcano.

Kauai, also known as the "Garden Isle," is filled with lush landscapes and pristine beaches backed by dramatic cliffs. Some of the highlights on this island include the Nā Pali Coast, Waimea Canyon State Park, and the quaint town of Hanalei.

Peak Hawaii Travel Times

As with most traveling, depending on your preferences, there isn't a better time than another to go to Hawaii. It comes down to your budget, your temperature preferences, and whether you're flexible about whether it will be sunny the entire time. It also depends on whether you want to be in the hustle and bustle of the crowds or if you want to visit when it's less busy. Here are some things to keep in mind in terms of travel seasons:

High season: High season in Hawaii is between mid-December to March. During this time, the weather is generally drier, and it coincides with winter in other parts of the world, making it a popular time for travelers to escape colder climates or for those who want to take a Christmas vacation. When traveling in these months, hotels may require a minimum stay, which is more expensive. You can also expect the demand for rental cars to be higher and the crowds will be busier at the attractions. Therefore, if you intend to travel during the high season, it's best to plan your itinerary accordingly.

Summer: Summer in Hawaii, from June to August, can also be a busy time to visit, especially for families traveling with children who are off from school. You can expect the weather to be hot and dry for the most part. However, hotels will generally be booked, and attractions will be busy.

Low season: If you want to avoid the crowds, consider visiting Hawaii between April and June or September to mid-December. During these months, you'll find the best deals on accommodations and fewer crowds at the attractions. However, it's worth noting that there's a higher chance of frequent rain if you travel during any of these months.

Month	Low temp	High temp
January	64 °F	81 °F
February	66 °F	81 °F
March	68 °F	82 °F
April	70 °F	84 °F
May	70 °F	86 °F
June	72 °F	88 °F
July	73 °F	88 °F
August	75 °F	90 °F
September	73 °F	90 °F
October	73 °F	88 °F
November	72 °F	84 °F
December	66 °F	82 °F

Flying to Hawaii Dos and Don'ts

Each of the significant islands has its own airports. So, when planning your trip to Hawaii, you'll want to choose the airport based on which island you want to be your "home base;" however, many travelers tend to choose Oahu as their main point. It's also important to note that some islands, like Maui and Big Island, have several different airports to choose from (which will be handy since you have to fly between the islands as there aren't any ferry services). To make this simplified, here are the five major airports that serve as gateways to Hawaii's islands:

Daniel K. Inouye International Airport (HNL): This airport is located on the island of Oahu in Honolulu. It is Hawaii's largest and busiest airport, as Oahu is the island most travelers choose as their entry point. This is a good option if you plan to stay in Oahu or if Oahu will be your final destination on your trip.

Kahului Airport (OGG): Located in Maui, this is Hawaii's second-busiest airport. It is a significant hub for inter-island travel and flights to the US mainland. This is an excellent airport if you're looking for budget-friendly and nonstop flights. However, don't choose this airport if you plan to stay near Hana or Kapulua. You'd better select the Hana Airport (HNM) or Kapalua Airport (JHM).

Ellison Onizuka Kona International Airport (KOA): Located on the west side of the Big Island, this airport is a crucial transportation hub for visitors coming to this Hawaiian island. Ellison Onizuka Kona International Airport offers direct flights to the US mainland and can connect you to other Hawaiian Islands. Don't choose this airport if you will be staying on the east side of the Big Island—you're better off flying into Hilo Airport (ITO).

Lihue Airport (LIH): Situated on the island of Kauai, this airport serves as the main gateway to Kauai and offers flights to other Hawaiian Islands and the US mainland. This is the only airport on this island, so if you're staying elsewhere, avoid flying into this island.

Lanai City Airport (LNY): Lanai City Airport is located on the island of Lanai. Lanai is one of the smaller Hawaiian Islands, which is great if you're looking for a low-key vacation rather than a bustling city vibe. But I won't recommend first timers to Hawaii to prioritize visit to Lanai.

Some other things to keep in mind about flying to Hawaii is that it can take upwards of 11 hours, depending on where you're flying from in the US and Canada on a direct flight; naturally, if you take nondirect flights, it will take longer to get to your final destination.

The next question is: Do you book your flight directly through the airline, or should you do it through a third-party travel agency? It all depends on your budget and what you are looking to do. The positive of booking your flight directly through the airline you want to fly with is that it eliminates any middle people. So, if you have an issue, you can deal with the airline company directly. On the other hand, it can be more expensive, and if you book it through a third-party travel agency or with a travel agent, you may find the best deals because you can package things.

Another thing to remember when booking your flights is to be flexible with travel dates. Certain days of the week will be more expensive to fly, whereas others, such as Tuesdays, Wednesdays, and Saturdays, tend to be cheaper. It also depends on the time you're planning to fly. Considering the time it takes to get to Hawaii, you're better off taking a late-night flight or red-eye, which is also cheaper. On the other hand, if you don't want to take a late-night flight but still want to save money, take an early-morning one.

Assuming you're still in the preliminary planning stages, you may also want to set notifications on Google Flights or Kayak to keep you updated on prices and future forecasts. Set these notifications at least six months before your travel dates to ensure you get the best price possible.

Visa and Document Requirements for Tourists

If you are a U.S. citizen, you only need to present a government photo I.D. However, you'll need your passport if you're flying in from an international destination, such as Canada or elsewhere.

Hawaii Packing Essentials

Given that Hawaii has a warm, tropical climate, there isn't a need for warm clothes unless you visit Haleakala National Park in Maui or Big Island in the winter. What your essential packing list should include

- shorts and T-shirts
- comfortable footwear for walking
- sandals
- swimsuit
- UV protective clothing
- sunglasses
- backpack
- mineral-based sunscreen that is coral reef friendly (Sun Bum is a great option)
- water bottle
- beach bag
- bug repellant (aim for something eco-friendly, such as Murphy's Naturals or Babyganics Travel Bug Spray)
- light rain jacket
- rash guard

If you plan to visit Hawaii in the winter months and intend to see some of the volcanoes, you can expect light snow on the summits. Therefore, to keep you warm

What NOT To Do - Hawaii

during those excursions, you'll want a sweatshirt, gloves, hat, sweatshirt, and a compressible down coat.

Handling All Things Currency in Hawaii

U.S. Citizens

If you are a U.S. citizen traveling to Hawaii, you won't need to worry about exchanging currency as everything is in U.S. Dollars ($).

Non-U.S. Citizens

If you are traveling from Canada or elsewhere, it's best to exchange currency before you travel, which can be done at your bank or a currency exchange location. They will have the most current exchange rate. If you forget or decide later that you want cash, try to avoid exchanging currency at an airport kiosk, as their exchange rates aren't the best (and you may end up delayed as you wait for other travelers trying to do the same thing).

Alternatively, if you don't want to carry cash, use your credit card when possible, as it almost always has the best exchange rate. However, you will want to check with your credit card provider or foreign exchange fees, which can add up quickly.

Travel and Car Rental Insurance

Travel insurance is not necessary but always recommended. It can cover flight delays or cancellations, lost luggage, health emergencies, stolen property, and other disruptions that can cause you to delay or cancel your trip. Additionally, as Hawaii is a chain of islands, it is sometimes subject to adverse weather conditions that can cause a natural disaster. So, travel insurance would be handy if you needed to be evacuated.

While shopping for travel insurance, it is worth investing in vehicle insurance if you intend to rent a car at any point. Depending on the type of insurance you get, it can cover

- collision damage or car theft
- liabilities
- accidents that cause injury to you and your passengers
- personal effects in the event your personal belongings are stolen from the car
- accidents with someone uninsured or underinsured

Remember to read the fine print about what your insurance will cover to avoid surprises when looking into these types of insurance.

Hawaii Travel Don'ts

Throughout this book, we will explore the things to avoid while visiting Hawaii's islands. Here are some things you should avoid while traveling or in Hawaii.

Don't Touch the Local Animals

When you see the animals, remember not to approach them or touch them. The turtles, specifically the green sea turtles, are protected. Enjoy the local animals from a distance, especially since it could land you with a hefty fine or even in jail!

Don't Touch or Disturb Coral

Coral reefs are essential ecosystems that play a critical role in the health and biodiversity of the ocean. Not only do they provide a habitat for diverse marine life, but they also support millions of species by serving as breeding grounds. Additionally, they act as natural barriers to protect coastlines by providing a buffer from the impact of storms and waves. Beyond their ecological importance, they hold significant economic value in creating medicine, food, and fishing opportunities. Therefore, don't touch the coral or step on it, as it can cause severe damage (and it can cut you badly).

Don't Wear Sunscreen That Isn't Reef Safe

On that note, to avoid disturbing the coral, you will want to wear reef-friendly sunscreen! You want to wear sunscreens that don't include harsh chemicals that will hurt the coral reef. Reef-friendly sunscreen will not include the following ingredients: oxybenzone, octinoxate, octocrylene, and parabens.

When shopping for reef-friendly sunscreens, look for the "reef-safe" label on the bottle.

Don't Call Everyone Hawaiian on the Island

Even though many people live in Hawaii, they are not classified as "Hawaiians." That term is reserved for those who are descendants of Native Hawaiians.

Don't Limit Your Travel Time

Hawaii has plenty of things to see and do; if you can, try to spend at least three days on each island. Your trip should be at least 10 days if you want to get the most out of it and ensure you make time to enjoy yourself! However, recognize that 10

What NOT To Do - Hawaii

days may not be enough and you likely won't see every island unless you're there for at least two and a half weeks.

Don't Ignore Safety

Hawaii's natural beauty can also pose risks, such as strong ocean currents, rough terrain, and unpredictable weather. Always heed warning signs, stay on marked trails, and follow safety guidelines provided by local authorities.

Don't Take Sand or Lava Rocks Home with You

An old legend says if you take a lava rock home with you, you'll be cursed from a Disney standpoint. When Maui stole the heart of Tahiti, it didn't bode well for the islands until Moana brought Maui to restore it. Leave it where it is.

The same goes for sand. Don't take it home! It protects the ecosystem and helps prevent erosion.

Don't Disrespect Local Cultural and Sacred Sites

When you are in Hawaii, treat it like you would back home. Ensure you follow protocols for local cultural sites so your fellow travelers can enjoy the island and its biodiversity. Likewise, when you visit sacred sites in Hawaii, such as temple ruins, burial grounds, and volcanoes, remember these are rooted in deep spiritual meaning, so don't remove or touch anything.

Don't Underestimate Travel Cost

Hawaii is more expensive than many other travel destinations within the US due to its remote location and high cost of living. Budget carefully and be prepared for higher-than-average prices for accommodations, dining, and activities.

Don't Forget to Rent a Car

While some areas like Waikiki may have excellent public transportation, many attractions are spread out across the islands. Renting a car allows for greater flexibility and accessibility.

Don't Underestimate Travel Time

Distances between attractions on the islands can be deceivingly far due to winding roads and traffic congestion. In some of the winding terrain, you won't be able to drive more than 25-30 miles per hour. Plan ample time for travel between destinations to avoid feeling rushed.

Don't Forget to Pack the Right Shoes and Clothing

You can expect to do plenty of walking in Hawaii, so pack the right shoes and clothing for your excursions.

Don't Forget to Prepare for Rain and Adverse Weather

While Hawaii is generally sunny, some months experience more rain and adverse weather than others. When packing for your trip, a good rule of thumb is to check the weather at least a week in advance so you know what to expect.

Don't Wear Shoes into Someone's Home

If you are visiting someone in Hawaii, remember to remove your shoes when entering their home. This is a Japanese tradition, and it is considered disrespectful if you walk in and around someone's house while still wearing your shoes.

Always Carry Some Cash

While credit cards are widely accepted in Hawaii, some smaller vendors, food trucks, and markets may only accept cash. Be sure to have some cash on hand for these situations, especially in more remote areas.

Don't go Overboard on the Planning Itinerary.

While it's tempting to fill your itinerary with activities and sightseeing, don't forget to schedule downtime for relaxation and rejuvenation. Take advantage of Hawaii's serene beaches, lush landscapes, and tranquil atmosphere to unwind and recharge.

Building Your Hawaiian Itinerary

Hawaii is a beautiful paradise with a surprisingly rich history in which to immerse yourself. The unique landscapes, diverse ecosystems, and sandy beaches sprawling for miles will make your trip unforgettable, no matter what you choose to do. Beginning to research for your trip is just the starting point. In the next chapter, we will start considering ways to build your itinerary for Hawaii, including how to get around and stay safe.

Chapter 2:

Tips and Tricks to Explore Hawaii

Do you know the history of the Hawaiian flag and why it consists of the Union Jack? The Hawaiian Flag dates back to the 1790s when Great Britain's Captain George Vancouver gifted King Kamehameha I with the Union Jack. This flag was Hawaii's unofficial flag until 1816 when Western advisors suggested the flag incorporate red, blue, and white stripes in addition to the Union Jack. These eight stripes reflect Hawaii's main islands: Big Island, Maui, Kaho'olawe, Lanai, Molokai, Ni'ihau, Kauai, and Oahu.

How to Get Around Hawaii

Getting around Hawaii will vary depending on the island on which you are starting your Hawaiian adventure. But one thing to note is that unless you take a multiday inter-island Hawaiian cruise, no ferry services will take you from one island to the next. Therefore, you will need to fly from one Hawaiian Island destination to the next. Otherwise, renting a car is the most convenient way to explore multiple attractions in Hawaii or adventure off the beaten path. Some things to keep in mind if you're driving:

- Obey the speed limit.
- Take the time to familiarize yourself with Hawaii's driving laws and regulations.
- Plan your travel times accordingly, especially if renting a car while on the Oahu island.
- Be mindful of the winding roads if you go off the beaten path.

Ride-sharing services like Uber and Lyft operate widely on the major islands and are a great option if you don't want to rent a car. Taxis are also an alternative but can be pricey if the trip is long.

Public transportation is available on Oahu and Maui if you're looking for a more budget-friendly option. In Oahu, their public transportation is called TheBus, which offers bus and train (Skyline) services to get you around the island. Maui also has a bus service that will take you to the main areas, including Lahaina, Ka'anapali, Kahului, Wailuku, and Kihei.

Fare type	TheBus (Oahu)	Maui Bus
Single fare (per person)	$3	$4
Day pass (per person)	$7.50	$4
7-day pass (per person)	$30	Not applicable
Seniors (55 and up), persons with a disability, and Medicare cardholders	Not applicable	$1
Children under 5	Free	Free

Money-saving hack: If you're going to be in Oahu and using their public transportation system, consider picking up a HOLO card, as your transportation will be $2 instead of $3.

Bicycling is another popular way to see the islands. If you opt to rent a bicycle, be sure you wear a helmet and obey the rules of the road, including riding single file on the roads, stopping at stop signs and red lights, and signaling your turns.

Staying Safe in Hawaii

Compared to the mainland U.S., Hawaii is considered relatively safe, with lower crime rates. However, like any destination, it's essential to exercise caution and be

What NOT To Do - Hawaii

aware of your surroundings. Ensure you lock your valuables in your hotel safe, don't leave your belongings unattended or in plain view in your rental car, and avoid secluded areas, especially at night.

Some common scams to be mindful of while in Hawaii include fake parking attendants and timeshare presentations that may leave you feeling coerced into making a purchase you didn't want to. While researching your trip, if you're looking for accommodations through Vrbo or Airbnb, thoroughly verify whether it is a legitimate listing. Sometimes prices are not what they seem!

Should you need to contact emergency services in Hawaii, 911 is the main number to call. The non-emergency phone number is (808) 935-3311.

Visitor Assistance

If you ever need visitor assistance due to adversity, call the Visitor Aloha Society of Hawaii (VASH)

- **Oahu:** (808) 926-8274
- **Kauai:** (808) 482-0111
- **Maui Visitors and Convention Bureau:** (808) 224-3530
- **Island of Hawaii—Kona:** (808) 756-0785
- **Island of Hawaii—Hilo:** (808) 756-1472

Hawaii Emergency Management Agency

You may hope your trip will be filled with sunny, blue skies, but you never know what Mother Nature may intend for your trip. If there is a weather emergency, be sure to tune into a radio station to find out more details:

- **Island of Hawaii (Big Island):** 670 AM, 850 AM, 94.7 FM, 97.9 FM, and 106.1 FM
- **Kauai:** 93.5 FM
- **Maui:** 550 AM
- **Oahu:** 590 AM, 92.3 FM, and 96.3 FM

Staying Safe on Land and in the Ocean

Hawaii is a paradise lover's oasis or an outdoor enthusiast's heaven. Before you embark on any outdoor adventure, research and plan accordingly—especially if you are not joining a tour company. You'll want to familiarize yourself with where you are going, including the trail, terrain, difficulty level, and potential hazards.

While hiking, remember to stay on the marked trails and designated paths, as venturing off-trail can impact the ecosystem, or you can wind up lost or injured. You will also want to stay weather-aware if you face an unpredictable weather pattern, especially in higher-elevation areas.

While enjoying the stunning coastal waters of the Pacific Ocean, ensure you prioritize your safety by swimming at beaches with lifeguards on duty. Before entering the water, you'll want to know the ocean conditions, including wave height and tide times. White, yellow, and red flags will also be posted to tell you whether or not swimming is safe:

- White flag: Calm conditions
- Yellow flag: Potential hazards, but fins are required due to strong currents or high waves
- Red flag: Unsafe to swim, and the beach will not be open

Traveling With Family or as a Solo Female

If you are planning a family vacation to Hawaii, it's essential to research and plan activities that can accommodate everyone's ages, interests, and physical abilities. When you arrive, ensure you establish a meeting point in case you get separated, especially at busier attractions. We'll cover some family-friendly options, but remembering this during the early planning stages is always a great idea!

On the other hand, if you're traveling as a solo female, trust your instincts—if something feels uncomfortable, remove yourself from the situation. Avoid walking alone at night. If you must, stick to well-lit and populated areas and consider using ride-sharing services or taxis for transportation.

Dos and Don'ts of Respecting Hawaiian Culture

Unlike U.S. mainland culture and etiquette, you will find it different in Hawaii and may find it challenging to adapt, even if your trip is only a week or two long! This section will focus on the dos and don'ts of respecting Hawaiian culture to blend in and connect yourself deeper to this state.

Understand the Difference Between Hawaiian Locals and a Hawaiian Person

If you were born or lived in New York City, you're likely referred to as a "New Yorker," so it's easy to assume that if someone lives in Hawaii, they are, by default, Hawaiian.

To be considered Hawaiian, their roots must be able to be traced back to their ancestors and native Hawaiians who inhabited the islands. Therefore, just because someone was born in Hawaii does not necessarily mean they are of Hawaiian descent; they are simply residents or locals.

Learn About Hawaii's History

Hawaii's culture is rich and beautiful, which is what makes this state so unique to the rest of the US. Learning more about it and staying curious are some of the best ways to learn about Hawaiian culture because it will not only connect you to its origins and to it becoming a part of the United States, but it also allows you to appreciate its vastly different culture compared to the mainland.

Cultivate the Aloha Spirit

Aloha is more than just a greeting in Hawaii—it's a concept that's taken seriously, to the point that it is a law in Hawaii. To everyone in Hawaii, aloha means taking care of one another and fostering a sense of inclusivity and community among those who live in Hawaii.

Remember to Tip

Tourism is a significant part of Hawaii's economy, with many residents depending on gratuity to make ends meet. When you dine out, visit a bar, join a tour guide, or take a taxi or rideshare, it is customary to tip between 15% and 20% for satisfactory service.

Pull Over to Let Cars Pass

When you venture off the beaten path, you will encounter plenty of twisty two-lane roads that may go down to a single lane in some areas. Keep an eye on your mirrors, and if you find someone following closely, pull over when you can so they can pass.

Support Local Businesses

You'll need groceries if you have opted to stay at a self-catering option in Hawaii. Hawaii does have plenty of big box stores, but sometimes going local is better! For one, it supports small businesses; two, you can mingle with a local; and three, you're helping the business owners support their families.

Remember Hawaii Is Sacred to Its People

A key aspect of respecting Hawaiian culture is to acknowledge and respect its roots to the native people who have lived here through years of generations. Remember to treat Hawaii as you would at someone else's home to ensure you respect Hawaiian cultures and traditions.

Respect Lei Etiquette

Leis have been a part of Hawaiian culture since the early Polynesian settlers inhabited the islands. Chiefs exchanged these symbols of peace among different groups, thus making these customary gifts an essential part of Hawaiian culture. When you are presented with a lei, graciously accept it and wear it when you are in the presence of the person giving it to you. To wear a lei properly, drape it around your neck and allow the flowers to hang in the front and back.

Respect the Hula Dance

The traditional hula dance is more than entertainment for visitors—it reflects Hawaii's deep culture and heritage. To Hawaiians, hula dancing holds significance as a powerful art form, deeply rooted in tradition and is worshiped by the local community. So, while you may be invited on stage to try it out, don't take it lightly or make fun of it.

Stay Humble and Always Ask for Permission

While in Hawaii, you may be judged based on your mannerisms. Avoid being flashy and arrogant, and stay kind when interacting with others.

On this same note, always be willing to ask questions or for permission around things you are unsure about, such as where to go or what to wear to something. If you're at a private residence or land, ask for permission before proceeding.

Participate in Authentic Hawaiian Experiences

When you visit Hawaii, seek opportunities to experience and connect with Native Hawaiian individuals to understand the local traditions and environment. You'll be given plenty of things to see and do, but in your planning, be sure to explore other options to experience, such as attending cultural gatherings organized by Hawaiians, joining an educational excursion that can teach you more about the Hawaiian heritage, and support local Hawaiian artists and businesses. Hula is one way to immerse yourself in the culture, but there is much more to do when you're open to it.

Be Respectful of Sensitive Topics

Specific topics in Hawaii are sensitive to some people, including the overthrow, annexation, and cultural losses. If they do come up for whatever reason, be thoughtful as you learn about someone's perspective.

Respect the Kupuna (Elders)

Hawaiian people have been taught much about respecting their kupunas (elders), and it's essential to demonstrate this even as a visitor. If you see an older person entering the same place you are, let them go first and hold doors open for them. If you're on public transportation, give up your seat.

Don't Try to Speak Pidgin English

English is a widely spoken language, but another official language in Hawaii is Pidgin English. This language is a fusion of different languages from those who moved to Hawaii throughout the centuries, including China, Japan, Korea, Portugal, the Philippines, and Europe. This unique language was used to communicate with the Hawaiian natives. Some key phrases you may hear include

- Howzit: What's up or aloha
- Da kine: Something you can't remember the name of
- Slippahs: Sandals or flip-flops

It sounds new-aged, but if you've never spoken Pidgin, don't try it.

Don't Park Illegally

One of the most significant complaints from the locals is the amount of people illegally parking along the roads, especially in popular areas of the islands. Be sure to adhere to parking regulations, and don't ignore signage telling you otherwise.

First Stop: Island of Hawaii

In this chapter, we explored the various ways to navigate Hawaii, how to stay safe, and the cultural etiquette while immersing yourself in their culture. Now that you have all the basics for planning your trip to Hawaii, it's time to start looking at the Hawaiian Islands, starting with the Island of Hawaii, best known as the Big Island.

Chapter 3:

Hawaii Island—Dos and Don'ts

Did you know the Island of Hawaii, the Big Island, was instrumental to NASA's Apollo program in the 1960s? The volcanic terrain and isolated environment of Mauna Kea was a perfect lunar-like setting for simulating the moon mission. The training involved practicing navigating the rugged landscapes by driving a "moon buggy," "sampling" rocks, and training on fresh lava flow. This helped the astronauts gear up for the historic moon missions, which was epic for that era! (Okay, let's be honest—it's still pretty neat when astronauts go out to space!)

Discovering the Island of Hawaii

The Island of Hawaii might be the youngest chain of islands in Hawaii. Still, it's undoubtedly the most impressive island because it measures about the same size as Connecticut! Nonetheless, visiting the Island of Hawaii will offer unlimited things to see and do on your Hawaiian journey as you explore the archaeological sites, volcanoes, and lush valleys that shape the Island of Hawaii's unique geography. Let's explore what you should do on the Big Island and the beaches to enjoy if you plan to venture over to this Hawaiian island.

What to Do on the Island of Hawaii

Hawaii Volcanoes National Park

Address: 1 Crater Rim Drive, Hawaii Volcanoes National Park, HI 96718

Hours of operation: The Kīlauea Visitor Center is open between 9 a.m. and 5 p.m. daily and is a great starting point for the park so that you can get any updated information about the trails or activities led by a park ranger.

Hawaii Volcanoes National Park is the most unique national park in the country, as it is home to two active volcanoes. This national park is a United Nations Educational, Scientific and Cultural Organization (UNESCO) World Heritage Site, and here you can witness the impressive sites of the Kilauea and Mauna Loa volcanoes that have continually reshaped the park's landscape.

Additionally, visitors can explore the Halema'uma'u crater, an active steaming crater within the summit of the Kilauea volcano. At one point, it was home to a lava lake and was a sacred site believed to be the home of Pele, the Hawaiian goddess of fire. In the last few years, Halema'uma'u has seen plenty of geological changes based on how the lava flows beneath the summit. It's always been an exciting site for scientists to explore and observe its changes and how it impacts the surrounding area. For visitors, it's impressive to see the size of the crater with steam coming from beneath it.

If you venture along Crater Rim Road, you'll find other top attractions, including the Devastation Trail. As the name suggests, you will see the devastation left in the wake of the 1959 eruption from the Iki crater. Another exciting attraction to explore is the Thurston Lava Tube. This is cool because the lava flowed through this area and weirdly cooled, creating a tunnel 20 feet high and 500 feet long.

Remember to pack a light jacket in your backpack if this will be on your destination list for your trip, as the summit can get cool!

Entrance type	What it includes	Price
Private vehicle	Admits the pass holder and up to 14 passengers in a private car.	$30
Motorcycle	Admins the pass holder and passenger of one motorcycle	$25
Per person	Admits one pedestrian, hiker, or bicyclist visiting the park without a private vehicle or motorcycle.	$15
Interagency pass	If you have this pass, you will be admitted to more than 2,000 federal recreation parks across the US.	Free if you have this pass. Otherwise, it is $80 to purchase.
Children under 5	Free	Free

All entrance fees must be paid by debit or credit card.

Akaka Falls State Park

Address: There is no official address for the Akaka Falls State Park. However, if you are Google mapping it and want to verify the zip code, it is 96728.

Hours of operation: 8:30 a.m. to 5 p.m. daily

Akaka Falls State Park is home to two of the Big Island's most famous waterfalls: the Akaka Falls and Kahuna Falls. Akaka is an impressive 442 feet high, making it the island's tallest waterfall. You'll enjoy the beautiful, lush scenery surrounding the waterfall with its tropical ferns, orchids, and bamboo. The hike to Akaka Falls is just under half a mile but has some steps, so it can be challenging for those with physical limitations. As you follow the trail to Akaka, you'll pass the Kahuna Falls as well.

Entrance type	**Price**
General Admission	$5
Children under 3	Free

If you are driving, the parking fees are as follows:

- Passenger vehicles with up to seven people: $25
- Passenger vehicles carrying 8 to 25 people: $50
- Passenger vehicles carrying 26 people or more: $90

Due to Akaka's limited cell reception, you're encouraged to pre-pay for parking if you are driving. You can do this through the ParkMobile app. The zone number is 808030.

Pu'uhonua o Honaunau National Historical Park

Address: State Hwy 160, Hōnaunau, HI 96726

Hours of operation: 8:30 a.m. to 4:30 p.m.

Pu'uhonua o Honaunau National Historical Park has a rich and historical significance in Hawaiian culture. This was once the place for refuge for those who broke sacred laws, also known as kapu. Those who broke the laws sought absolution and protection within these sacred walls, where they could find redemption and forgiveness under the guidance of priests.

You can explore restored structures, stone walls, and a sanctuary at this park. There is also the landing palace, where the royal canoes would dock to see, and replica wood carvings of temple gods placed where the original statues once were.

Entrance type	What it includes	Price
Private vehicle	Admits the pass holder and up to 14 passengers in a private car.	$20
Motorcycle	Admins the pass holder and passenger of one motorcycle	$15
Per person	Admits one pedestrian, hiker, or bicyclist visiting the park without a private vehicle or motorcycle.	$10
Interagency pass	If you have this pass, you will be admitted to more than 2,000 federal recreation parks across the US.	Free if you have this pass. Otherwise, it is $80 to purchase.

What NOT To Do - Hawaii

Pololū Valley Lookout

Address: 52-5100 Akoni Pule Hwy, Kapaau, HI 96755

Hours of operation: The lookout is open all year round. For the best pictures, go for sunrise or later in the evening.

Pololū Valley Lookout offers a breathtaking view of the Big Island's stunning natural landscapes. At this lookout point, you will see beautiful views of the rugged coastline of the Hamakua coast, cliffs covered with lush greenery, leading down to the black sandy beach and the Pololū Valley below. It's worth following the Awini trail down as you can see the Pololū stream, which leads right into the Pacific Valley, rope swings, and even some cows eating the grass in the distant meadows.

Beyond the stunning scenery, the valley holds significance in Hawaiian culture and history, as this was where King Kamehameha was born. Additionally, Pololū Valley was once an important settlement and agricultural area for the early inhabitants of Hawaii up until the early 1900s.

This lookout is a free attraction, and you should plan to spend at least a few hours here if you intend to hike down and back (which is just under a mile).

Hawaii Tropical Botanical Garden

Address: 27-717 Mamalahoa Hwy, Papaikou, HI 96781

Hours of operation: The botanical gardens are open from 9 a.m. to 5 p.m. daily, except for major holidays. (The last entry is at 4 p.m.)

Located atop Onomea Bay, the Hawaii Tropical Botanical Garden is a lush paradise filled with diverse flora from around the globe within its 40-acre tropical

rainforest. At this botanical garden, you will see a collection of over 2,500 plant species, including 200 species of palm and extinct plants.

Ticket type	Price
Adults	$30
Active military (with valid ID)	$25
Children (6 to 12 years old)	$22
Children under 6	Free

Ahu'ena Heiau

Address: Kaahumanu Pl, Kailua-Kona, HI 96740

Ahu'ena Heiau is behind the Kamehameha Hotel and is one of the most important sites on the Big Island. This temple was where King Kamehameha spent the final years of his life. Following Kamehameha's death, his son, Liholiho, became the next king and started the Lahaina, a form of government.

You won't be able to go inside the building physically. However, you should visit the hotel lobby, where you can see several artifacts and portraits of former Hawaiian royalty.

Kaumana Caves

Address: 1492 Kaumana Dr, Hilo, HI 96720

The Kaumana Caves in Hilo give you a unique opportunity to explore a natural wonder created by the Mauna Loa volcano when it erupted sometime in the 19th century. This is one of the best spots in Hawaii to explore caves, especially if you're traveling with family.

If you do intend to go deeper into the caves, here are some things to keep in mind:
- Wear a headlamp because it gets dark fast!
- If you are going to wander a little further into the cave without a headlamp or flashlight, don't go further than where the light from the outside reaches.
- Wear running shoes as the cave is slippery.
- Don't carve your initials or anything else into the lava rocks.

The Island of Hawaii Beaches

Hapuna Beach State Park

Address: Old Puako Rd, Waimea, HI 96743

Hapuna Beach State Park is the most popular beach option on the Big Island for its beautiful white sand and calm waters, and it is excellent for snorkeling and boogie boarding (also known as bodyboarding). This beach also has lifeguards, picnic tables in a shaded area, and food and beverages for sale. If you intend to spend the day here, come early because it can get crowded and make it hard to find a shady spot for your beach blanket!

Kaunaoa Beach

Address: 62-100 Mauna Kea Beach Dr, Puako, Hawaii

Kaunaoa Beach, also known as Mauna Kea Beach due to its being along the Mauna Kea Beach Hotel Property, is along the Kohala Coast. This beach is well-known and appreciated for its white sand and calm waters within its crescent-shaped bay. If you go to either end, you'll see a ton of reefs that protect the beach, making for a great snorkeling excursion. (Remember the rule of not disturbing them!)

Coming here at night is also an exciting excursion as the hotel will flood the waters with light to attract plankton, a stingray's favorite meal! You'll see the stingrays glide through the water to get their fill, which is a neat experience, especially with kids! The hotel also offers nighttime scuba and snorkeling sessions.

To access this beach, you will need to go through Mauna Kea Resort. There are limited parking spaces for those not staying at the hotel, and parking is $21. When you approach the gate attendant, tell them you're going to the beach. On the other hand, if you are staying at the resort, you will need to get a beach access card from the front desk. Additionally, this beach does not have a lifeguard.

Anaehoomalu Beach

Address: 69-275 Waikōloa Beach Dr, Waikoloa Village, HI 96738

Anaehoomalu Beach, also called A-Bay, is a stunning golden beach along the Kohala Coast. This is an excellent beach for recreational activities such as stand-up paddleboarding, kayaking, canoeing, hydro bicycling, swimming, and snorkeling. In addition to enjoying the beach and the recreational activities it has to offer, there are a pair of ponds with historical significance. These ponds, named Ku'uali'i and Kahapapa, were ponds used by the royals to raise small fish and mullets. If you venture over to see these, please note that there is no swimming in the ponds. Additionally, you can follow the King's Trail, which will take you to other historical and ancient sites.

This beach also has convenient amenities, including picnic areas, restrooms, showers, and changing rooms.

Punalu'u Black Sand Beach

Address: Ninole Loop Rd, Naalehu, Hawaii

Punalu'u Black Sand Beach is a unique beach on the Island of Hawaii. The sand has granular lava mixed into it, giving it its black look along the shoreline and an interesting contrast against the turquoise waters. If you plan to visit this beach, it's advisable to check the water conditions as the currents can be strong at times. However, there are lifeguards at this beach to inform visitors if the waters are safe.

Additionally, as the sand is black, it absorbs the heat, so wear proper sandals to prevent severe burns. You may also see green sea turtles warming up on the beach or swimming in the waters. Remember to keep your distance if you see one.

Kekaha Kai State Park

Address: HI-19, Kailua-Kona, HI 96740

Kekaha Kai State Park spans 1,600 acres of beautiful, golden sandy beaches with crystal-clear turquoise waters. There are several beaches to enjoy at this state park, all with several fish you can see if you snorkel. There are also barbecues, restrooms, showers, and shaded picnic areas to use here.

What Events to Enjoy on the Island of Hawaii

Depending on when you'll be in Hawaii, you can expect to find plenty of events to enjoy. This book will cover some of the events on each respective island. Here is what you can check out if you are on the Island of Hawaii.

Merrie Monarch Festival

The Merrie Monarch Festival is a week-long festival held yearly starting on Easter Sunday. This event has been around since 1963 and is considered one of the most prestigious hula competitions in the world, famous for its celebration of Hawaiian culture, music, and dance. However, it's more than just a competition. Its goal is to preserve hula's ancient art and honor King Kalakaua I.

At this event, you can expect to see plenty of people competing in a hula competition, which takes place over three of the seven days. There is also a crafts fair and live musical performances to immerse yourself further in Hawaiian culture.

If you are planning to attend the hula competition, there is a maximum number of two tickets per purchaser, ranging from $10 to $55, depending on whether you want general admission or reserved seating. The crafts fair is free to attend.

Ka'ū Coffee Festival

If you love coffee, this is an excellent festival for you! The Ka'ū Coffee Festival is a vibrant celebration of the Island of Hawaii's rich coffee-growing heritage dating back to the late 19th century. This festival happens annually and brings residents, farmers, and coffee enthusiasts together, highlighting the vital role of coffee farming in the Ka'ū agricultural economy while maintaining sustainable farming practices.

- There are plenty of events to enjoy, including

- sampling coffees.
- challenging yourself with a free cooking contest.
- attending the Pa'ina and open house at the Pahala Plantation House (free).
- taking a self-guided tour of the Ka'ū Coffee Farms.
- joining the Ka'ū mountain hike and lunch ($60 per person).
- learning more about the descendants of the first coffee farmer in Ka'ū at the Ka'ū coffee and cattle day at the Aikane Plantation Coffee Farm ($35 per person).
- start watching at the Ka'ū coffee mill ($60 per person).
- attending the main event, Ho'olaule'a, where you can enjoy hula, live music, local food, crafts, coffee tours, and more!

You will want to check their website for official dates as they change yearly.

Annual Farm Festival at Hāmākua Harvest

The Annual Farm Festival at Hāmākua Harvest is a festival that celebrates local agriculture, sustainable farming practices, and community resilience. This festival starts with the Honoka'a Western Week in May to highlight the Paniolo culture. During this event, you can join educational presentations (some of which are hands-on), enjoy food from local vendors, and shop at a farmers market.

Kona Brewers Festival

The Kona Brewers Festival is an annual beer festival held in Kailua-Kona. This is a great festival if you love craft beer, as you can taste craft beers from around Hawaii and enjoy food made with locally sourced ingredients. In addition, the Ke Kai Ala Foundation, which hosts this festival, aims to raise money to help nonprofit organizations focused on environmental protection and conservation, support the youth, and preserve Hawaii's culture.

Please note that beer tastings are only available to those 21 and over.

Ticket type	Price
General admission (8 beer-tasting tokens and a souvenir-tasting glass)	$50
Connoisseur pass (10 beer-tasting tokens, lanyard koozie, food and beer samples, and a T-shirt or hat)	$150

Where to Eat on the Island of Hawaii

Hawaiian Style Café

Address

- Hilo location: 681 Manono Street, Suite 101, Hilo, HI 96720
- Waimea location: 65-1290 Kawaihae Road, Kamuela, HI 96743

Hours of operation

Day of the week	Hilo	Waimea
Monday	7 a.m. to 2 p.m.	7 a.m. to 1:30 p.m.
Tuesday	7 a.m. to 2 p.m. and 5 p.m. to 8:30 p.m.	7 a.m. to 1:30 p.m.
Wednesday	7 a.m. to 2 p.m. and 5 p.m. to 8:30 p.m.	7 a.m. to 1:30 p.m.
Thursday	7 a.m. to 2 p.m. and 5 p.m. to 8:30 p.m.	7 a.m. to 1:30 p.m.
Friday	7 a.m. to 2 p.m. and 5 p.m. to 9 p.m.	7 a.m. to 1:30 p.m.
Saturday	7 a.m. to 2 p.m. and 5 p.m. to 9 p.m.	7 a.m. to 1:30 p.m.
Sunday	7 a.m. to 2 p.m.	7 a.m. to 12 p.m.

The Hawaiian Style Café is a popular budget-friendly meal option with two locations to serve you. This café serves generous portions of all of your basic meals in addition to authentic Hawaiian cuisine, including family-made stews, Hawaiian and sweet bread, and French toast. Visitors of this restaurant love how flavorful the dishes are and the amount of food you get for the price.

Hilo Bay Café

Address: 123 Lihiwai St, Hilo, HI

Hours of operation: Hilo Bay Café is open from Tuesday to Sunday between 11 a.m. and 2:30 p.m. for lunch and from 5 p.m. to 8:30 p.m. for dinner.

The Hilo Bay Café is a popular place to eat among the locals on the Island of Hawaii due to its creative menu selection. At this café, you'll find a diverse menu of seafood and sushi to burgers and salads. Additionally, people love eating at Hilo Bay Café for its warm atmosphere and beautiful ocean views. It's recommended to make a reservation as tables fill up fast!

Kona Brewing Company

Address: 74-5612 Pawai Pl, Kailua Kona, HI 96740

Hours of operation: 10 a.m. to 9 p.m. daily

Kona Brewing Company is a father-son-owned company on the Big Island that has been operating for over 25 years. You can enjoy delicious craft-made beers made sustainably alongside traditional Hawaiian meals or hand-tossed pizzas at this brewery.

Umekes Fish Market Bar and Grill

Address: 74-5599 Pawai Pl, Kailua-Kona, HI 96740

Hours of operation: 11 a.m. to 9 p.m. daily

Umekes Fish Market Bar and Grill is a budget-friendly option for those who want to try a poke bowl or a fusion of a poke bowl. Owned and operated by Chef Nakoa Pabre, you can expect the bowls to be made with the freshest ingredients, all of which you can customize to your tastes.

Da Poke Shack

Address: 76-6246 Ali'i Dr, Suite 101, Kailua-Kona, HI 96740

Hours of operation: 10 a.m. to 4 p.m. (unless they sell out for the day)

Da Poke Shack is another popular establishment for getting a Poke Bowl. All bowls are made with the freshest ingredients and freshly caught yellowfin tuna (ahi). If you're not a fan of raw fish, they can substitute for traditional lau lau (fatty pork and butterfish in la'au and ti leaves) or pulled pork. They also have gluten-free and vegetarian options.

Holuakoa Café

Address: 76-5900 Old Government Rd, Holualoa, Island of Hawaii, HI 96725

Hours of operation

Monday to Friday: 10 a.m. to 2:30 p.m. and 5:30 p.m. to 8:30 p.m.

Saturday and Sunday: 9 a.m. to 2:30 p.m. and 5:30 p.m. to 8:30 p.m.

Holuakoa Café in Holualoa is a well-loved restaurant known for its farm-to-table meals and tranquility. Set in a historic building surrounded by gorgeous foliage, this restaurant focuses on creating meals with sustainably sourced ingredients that burst with flavor, reflecting Hawaii's agricultural diversity. This is an excellent spot to eat for a memorable dining experience.

Big Island Brewhaus

Address: 64-1066 Hawai'i Belt Rd, Waimea, HI 96743

Hours of operation: 11 a.m. to 9 p.m. daily

If there is one thing Tom and his wife, Jayne, appreciate, it's delicious food paired with craft beer. Big Island Brewhaus opened its doors to the public in March 2011 and has been creating a wide selection of craft beers and a diverse menu of pub fare for people to enjoy throughout the years. The prices for their food are budget-friendly and made with the freshest ingredients whenever possible.

Brown's Beach House

Address: 1 North Kaniku Dr, Kohala Coast, HI 96743

Hours of operation: 5:30 p.m. to 8:30 p.m. daily

This is a more expensive option, but great if you're looking for a nice night out on the island. Brown's Beach House offers stunning ocean views for your dining experience as you enjoy a wide range of menu options, from seafood to premium cuts of meat, all cooked with some of the best flavors from the region. If you intend to book a Brown's Beach House reservation, you must leave a credit card number with them.

Village Burger Waimea

Address: 67-1185 Hawai'i Belt Rd, Waimea, HI 96743

Hours of operation: 10:30 a.m. to 5 p.m. daily

Village Burger Waimea has built a reputation on the Island of Hawaii for its mouthwatering burgers, all created with top-quality ingredients. People love this restaurant for the flavors and care that goes into making the burgers, sides, and condiments to accompany your burger.

One Aloha Shave Ice Co.

Address: 75-5711 Kuakini Hwy, Kailua-Kona, HI 96740

Hours of operation: 12 a.m. to 5 p.m., Tuesday to Saturday

Shave ice is a specialty in Hawaii, and your trip wouldn't be complete without trying it at least once! All flavors are made daily from scratch and in small batches. The best part is that this establishment uses simple ingredients in all their treats!

What to Eat on the Island of Hawaii

Lū'au

A traditional Hawaiian feast, a lū'au typically features a variety of dishes, including kalua pig (slow-roasted pork cooked in an underground oven called an imu), lomi lomi salmon (a refreshing salad made with salted salmon, tomatoes, and onions), poi (a starchy dish made from taro root), and haupia (a coconut milk-based dessert).

Poke:

A popular Hawaiian dish made with cubed raw fish (usually ahi tuna or salmon) marinated in soy sauce, sesame oil, green onions, and other seasonings. Poke bowls are often served over rice or salad greens and can be customized with various toppings like avocado, seaweed, or tobiko (flying fish roe).

Loco Moco:

A hearty Hawaiian comfort food, loco moco typically consists of a base of white rice topped with a hamburger patty, a fried egg, and brown gravy. Variations may include adding spam, Portuguese sausage, or kimchi to the dish.

Kalua Pork:

A staple of Hawaiian cuisine, kalua pork is tender, smoky, and flavorful. Traditionally cooked in an underground oven (imu) or slow-roasted in an oven, the pork is seasoned with salt and often served shredded with cabbage, rice, or poi.

Malasadas:

A delicious Portuguese-inspired treat, malasadas are deep-fried doughnuts rolled in sugar and filled with various fillings such as custard, chocolate, or fruit preserves. These light and fluffy pastries are a favorite dessert or snack enjoyed by locals and visitors alike.

Where to Stay on the Island of Hawaii

Volcano House and Namakanipaio Campground

Address: 1 Crater Rim Dr, Hawaii Volcanoes National Park, HI 96718

Can't get enough of Volcanoes National Park? You can stay at the Volcanoes House within the park on the edge of the Kilauea volcano crater in one of their ten cabins. Staying at this accommodation will give you views of the active volcano in continuous eruption, which is both thrilling and a fantastic experience.

The Namakanipaio Campground is three miles from the Volcano House if you want to camp. Here, you also have the option to stay in one of their ten cabins, or you can rent a campsite equipped with a tent the staff will set up for you. If you opt to camp, the maximum stay is seven days.

Both of these options are great for those looking for budget-friendly options.

Kona Seaside Hotel

Address: 75-5646 Palani Rd, Kailua Kona, Kailua, HI 96740

Kona Seaside Hotel offers a budget-friendly stay without compromising on location or amenities. This hotel is steps away from the bustling Ali'i Drive and is close to shops, attractions, and restaurants.

This hotel has bright, spacious rooms (some overlook the ocean) and a pool to enjoy. There are no daily resort fees, which is a bonus if you try to stick to a budget.

Royal Kona Resort

Address: 75-5852 Ali'i Dr, Kailua-Kona, HI 96740

Royal Kona Resort is a three-star hotel with a saltwater lagoon, a private beach, and an outdoor swimming pool. Plenty of room options suit your traveling needs, including rooms with ocean views that can fit up to four people. If you're looking for some spa time, the Royal Kona Resort also has these services for an additional cost.

Shell Vacations Club Kona Coast Resort

Address: 78-6842 Ali'i Dr, Kailua-Kona, HI 96740

Shell Vacations Kona Coast Resort is a self-catering option in 21 lush tropical gardens. This resort is perfect for those traveling with families or couples looking for comfort and convenience. All villas have a kitchen, separate living and dining rooms, and a private balcony. Two pools are on-site, including a children's pool, tennis courts, volleyball courts, a fitness center with stunning panoramic ocean views, and barbecue areas throughout the resort. There are also on-site activities, such as hula lessons and diving. If you are renting a car, parking is free.

The Inn at Kulaniapia Falls

Address: 100 Kulaniapia Dr, Hilo, HI 96720

The Inn at Kulaniapia Falls is a luxury option sitting within 22 acres of lush greenery near the stunning Kulaniapia waterfall. You can rent a bungalow or a room that overlooks the garden, ocean, or waterfall. This tranquil resort has plenty of activities you can join, including rappelling tours of the Kulaniapia Falls. You can also go hiking on the trails in the area or rent a kayak and go kayaking.

Hilo Bay Oceanfront Bed and Breakfast

Address: 56 Pukihae St, Hilo, HI 96720

Hilo Bay Oceanfront Bed and Breakfast is an excellent retreat for travelers looking for a tranquil place to stay. This beautiful bed and breakfast is set in a home from the 1920s and has rooms that overlook the ocean. It is also near several of the popular attractions in the area, including the Hawaii Tropical Botanical Garden. Previous guests have all spoken highly of the owners and loved having breakfast while watching the sunrise. This bed and breakfast costs around $200 to $250 per night.

Hilo Reeds Bay Hotel

Address: 175 Banyan Dr, Hilo, HI 96720

Hilo Reeds Bay Hotel is in the center of Hilo and offers affordable and comfortable accommodations for your stay on the Island of Hawaii. This hotel is mid-range, and most rooms overlook the ocean. They also have a kitchenette in the rooms and are near the Hawaii Volcanoes National Park and the Kaūmana Caves.

Fairmont Orchid

Address: 1 North Kaniku Dr, Kohala Coast, HI 96743

Fairmont Orchid is another great luxury option for those seeking a serene retreat with stunning ocean views. This hotel is well-known for its world-class service and amenities to provide an unforgettable holiday. This hotel offers spa treatments, a swimming pool, an on-site golf course, and the Brown's Beach House restaurant for fine dining.

Kohala Village Inn

Address: 55-514 Hawi Rd, Hawi, HI 96719

Located in the heart of Hawaii, a historic town on the tip of the Island of Hawaii, Kohala Village Inn offers a charming retreat steeped with rustic charm. This charming inn has a laid-back atmosphere with picturesque surroundings of North Kohala. This is a great place to stay if you want an authentic Hawaiian experience, especially as you explore the town. Guests have highly rated this accommodation for the friendly staff.

Aston Kona by the Sea

Address: 75-6106 Ali'i Dr, Kailua-Kona, HI 96740

Aston Kona by the Sea is a higher-range option and puts you close to several of the nearby attractions on the island. The resort is a self-catering option with a fully-equipped kitchen. Guests can use the facility's oceanfront pool, hot tub, or barbecues.

What Not to Do on the Island of Hawaii

Don't Forget to Check if Volcanoes Are Active Before Going

Aside from Hawaii being a tropical paradise, many travel to the state hoping to witness the volcanoes and their lava. However, Mother Nature always has her plans, and you may not be able to see the volcanoes on your list. Always do your research beforehand to ensure there are no active volcanoes. Even then, marveling at this wonder while inactive is a sight!

Venturing Off-Trail in Volcanoes National Park

Stay on designated trails and overlooks to avoid damaging delicate volcanic landscapes and risking injury from unstable terrain. Do not attempt to approach active lava flows or enter restricted areas, as they pose serious risks of burns, toxic gases, and sudden collapses.

Don't Bring Pets while Visiting Akaka Falls State Park

Pets are not allowed on the trails or in the park, as they can disturb wildlife and pose safety risks to both animals and visitors. Pets are also not allowed in other state parks. Please check the park's guidelines for pets before visiting.

Don't Remove Artifacts in Honaunau National Park

Do not disturb or remove any artifacts, rocks, or shells from the park, as they are protected by law and hold cultural significance.

Don't Venture beyond the Fenced Area at Pololu Valley

Stay within designated viewing areas and avoid crossing safety barriers or venturing too close to cliff edges, as the terrain can be unstable and hazardous.

Don't Ignore Safety Warnings at Kaumana Caves

Heed warning signs and advisories related to cave conditions, including slippery surfaces, low ceilings, and potential hazards like loose rocks or falling debris. Always explore the caves with a buddy or in a group, as it can be easy to get disoriented or lost in the dark passages. Avoid touching or damaging cave formations such as stalactites, stalagmites, and flowstone, as they are delicate and take thousands of years to form. Bring a reliable flashlight or headlamp with extra batteries, sturdy shoes with good traction, and appropriate clothing for exploring the caves. Check for any closure notices or restrictions before visiting, as caves may be closed temporarily for safety reasons or to protect bat populations.

Don't Touch Sea Turtles at Punalu'u Black Sand Beach

While Punalu'u is known for its sea turtle population, it's important to keep a safe distance and avoid approaching or touching them, as they are protected by law, and disturbance can be harmful. Also, please refrain from taking sand from the beach as a souvenir, as it can contribute to erosion and disrupt the natural ecosystem.

Don't Forget to Be Mindful of These Areas

Everywhere you go, there are always areas to be mindful of visiting (or avoiding altogether):

- **Waianae:** Waianae has the highest homeless population and, as a result, there is a lot of crime in this town. There are also not a lot of places to stay or

things to do in this part of the island, so it's best to avoid visiting this spot. If you do find yourself here, exercise caution and avoid the beaches.
- **Waimea**: Aside from going to enjoy a burger at the delicious Village Burger Waimea, consider this town as a drive-by for the most part. Outside a couple of events—the Waimea Cherry Blossom Heritage Festival and the annual rodeo—there isn't much to do.
- **Pahoa**: At one point, Pahoa was a popular area for surfing until a volcano leveled out the area. Unfortunately, this town is home to a lot of sex offenders and sees plenty of theft.

Don't Swim Alone

This is obvious, but you want to be safe while swimming! Sure, you might be a strong swimmer, but the last thing you want to do is get caught by a shark or a massive wave. Always swim when there is a lifeguard on duty to ensure your safety.

Don't Go Hiking Unprepared

When hiking in Hawaii, you must prepare before heading out on the trails. This means ensuring your phone is charged and you have plenty of water and snacks and a first aid kit. It's also advisable to let your family know your itinerary and if you are going hiking in the event something happens.

Next Stop: The Island of Maui

The island of Hawaii has seen many things over its thousands of years, from volcanic eruptions to the creation of its lands or continually changing the island's shape to being the place for NASA to train for its moon missions in the 1960s. On Big Island, you can explore its diverse geography, including the lush rainforests of the Hawaii Tropical Botanical Garden and Akaka Falls, experience Hawaiian culture through the various events held throughout the year, and enjoy a beach day on one of the popular beaches.

In the next chapter, we will head to the Island of Maui to explore some of these island attractions, beaches, and things you should avoid.

Chapter 4:

Maui Island —Dos and Don'ts

If you have children or are a Disney fan, chances are you've watched Moana at least once. As we know, Maui is the demigod in the movie. But did you know there is some legend behind the Disney character? Legend has it that Maui is an actual demigod from Polynesian mythology. He earned his reputation when he lassoed the sun to dictate its movement to allow for more daylight on the island and increase fishing and agricultural activities for its inhabitants.

As Maui would say, "What can I say, except you're welcome" (Musker & Clements, 2016).

Discovering the Island of Maui

The enchanting island of Maui is famous for its stunning blend of landscapes, history, mythology, culture, and iconic landmarks. Like the other chain of islands

What NOT To Do - Hawaii

in Hawaii, Maui has seen plenty of fascinating life, from volcanoes to the ancient life of the Polynesian settlers and Hawaiian royalty. On this island, you can uncover Maui's past in many archaeological sites and sacred temples or join an event celebrating Hawaiian traditions.

Maui's stunning geography is backdropped by beautiful beaches with crystal-clear turquoise waters, dramatic cliffs, and some of the greenest rainforests in the world, leaving the door open for endless opportunities for exploration and outdoor adventures. Among some celebrated landmarks to explore, including the Haleakalā National Park and Road to Hana, plenty of quaint little towns are sprinkled throughout the island. This packed island has so much to see, so let's get right into it!

What to Do on the Island of Maui

Kapalua Coastal Trail

It's difficult to pick all the best hiking trails in Maui because there are so many! However, the Kapalua Coastal Trail is worth doing if you want a novice-level hike. This picturesque hike begins at Kapalua Bay Beach or D.T. Fleming Beach and is a 1.76-mile long roundtrip. It will offer you beautiful views of the Pacific Ocean, where you can see the waves crashing into the rugged lava rock formations, fields, gorgeous green spaces, and forests. This hike also allows you to watch for wildlife, including sea turtles, seabirds, seals, and whales (if you're there during winter when they come closer to land). Along the way, you can explore hidden coves and beaches, cultural landmarks, such as the Honokahua Preservation Site that dates back to 610, and the iconic Honolua Bay. If you park at the D.T. Fleming Beach parking lot, it is open from sunrise to sunset.

Along this trail, you will also encounter a couple of connection points for other hikes. One of these is the Mahana Ridge Trail, a challenging 10.4-mile hike. This one does begin at D.T. Fleming Beach and ends at the Maunalei Arboretum. This hike brings you up 2,000 feet in elevation, but the views from the top are worth it! The other hiking trail you can do from the Kapalua Coastal Trail is the Village Walking Trails, which has six different trails with different difficulties—some will have steeper hills than others.

Whatever hike you decide to do, whether just following the Kapalua Trail or branching off to explore the other two options, remember to wear proper footwear and bring water!

Haleakalā National Park

Dominating the landscape of Maui is the Haleakalā National Park. This impressive crater stands tall in the sky at about 10,023 feet above sea level and can be seen from nearly every island corner. This inactive volcano has 30,000 acres of terrain for outdoor adventure, taking you through beautiful rainforests home to thousands of native Hawaiian flora, fauna species, animals, and stunning waterfalls and streams. You'll even find some areas that resemble the sand an astronaut would see on Mars.

What NOT To Do - Hawaii

There are many reasons why people visit this state park, but it's the draw of watching the sunrise and sunset from its summit that makes for stunning photos. If you intend to do this, you'll want to give yourself at least 1.5 to 2.5 hours to drive to the top. It may be a super early start to your day, but I promise it will be well worth the drive and lack of sleep! For this excursion, you will need to reserve your spot in advance. However, if you don't want to wake up crazy early, you can still watch the sunset from the summit, too (and you don't need a reservation for that).

Entrance type	What it includes	Price
Private vehicle	Admits the pass holder and up to 14 passengers in a private car.	$30
Motorcycle	Admins the pass holder and passenger of one motorcycle	$25
Per person	Admits one pedestrian, hiker, or bicyclist visiting the park without a private vehicle or motorcycle.	$15
Sunrise viewing reservation	Reservation to watch the sunrise. This does not include entry into the park.	$1
Interagency pass	If you have this pass, you will be admitted to more than 2,000 federal recreation parks across the US.	Free if you have this pass. Otherwise, it is $80 to purchase.
Saturday	7 a.m. to 2 p.m. and 5 p.m. to 9 p.m.	7 a.m. to 1:30 p.m.
Sunday	7 a.m. to 2 p.m.	7 a.m. to 12 p.m.

Wai'anapanapa State Park

Address: Hana, HI 96713 (near mile marker 32)
Hours of operation: 7 a.m. to 6 p.m. daily

Wai'anapanapa State Park is situated along the beautiful Hana Coast and is a breathtaking oasis home to dense vegetation, rugged coastlines, and gorgeous black sand beaches formed by the eruption of volcanoes thousands of years ago. This state park is perfect for all outdoor enthusiasts and history buffs. Many trails will lead you to scenic viewpoints, ancient Hawaiian burial grounds, stone arches, caves, lava tubes where you can hear the ocean crashing into the land, and some blowholes.

If you plan to visit on a day pass, the entrance fee per person is $5 (free for children 3 and under), and parking fees are $10. If you intend to camp at this state park, campgrounds are $30 per night. Alternatively, you can rent a cabin, which is $100 per night. Cabin reservations must be online at least a week before your check-in date.

Maui Ocean Center

Address: 92 Māʻalaea Rd, Wailuku, HI 96793
Hours of operation: The park is open from 9 a.m. to 5 p.m. daily, with the last admission at 4 p.m. On Thanksgiving and Christmas Eve, Maui Ocean Center is open from 9 a.m. to 4 p.m., with the last admission at 3 p.m. If you plan to catch a show at the 3D Sphere Experience, performances begin at 10 a.m. and run every half hour throughout the day, with the last at 4:30 p.m. and at 3:30 p.m. on Thanksgiving and Christmas Eve.

Prepare to immerse yourself at the Maui Ocean Center to learn about the ocean's wonders. This ocean center is in a state-of-the-art facility. It offers diverse activities, from watching the colorful fish swimming in colorful tropical displays to watching the stingrays gracefully swim. There's even shark diving if you're brave! However, if diving with the sharks is not something you're looking to do, you can walk along the 35-foot-long acrylic tunnel as the sharks swim overhead, which makes for incredible photos!

For other exciting experiences at the Maui Ocean Center, you can go on a snorkeling tour with a marine biologist to see and learn about the coral reefs. There are yoga classes after hours in the acrylic tunnel if you want to practice yoga while the sharks and fish swim around and above you. There is also a plant tour where you can learn about the different plants in Hawaii and their importance. There is also a behind-the-scenes tour, which will show you how the staff care for the animals on site. If you plan to do the behind-the-scenes tour, it is an hour long and runs on Mondays, Wednesdays, Thursdays, and Fridays between 11:30 a.m. and 12:30 p.m. and from 1:30 p.m. to 2:30 p.m.

In addition to the experiences, there are several exhibits to explore, including.

- The turtle lagoon is where you can learn how marine biologists care for the endangered green turtle species and help prepare them for their journey in the wild.
- The living reef exhibit will allow you to see coral reefs at different ocean levels.
- The open ocean exhibit is where you can learn more about the importance of sharks and stingrays in our oceans.
- the various marine life displays.

To make the most of your day, it's recommended that you spend at least three hours here exploring everything the Maui Ocean Center has to offer.

For all ticket purchases, it is best to do it online.

Visitor Admission Only

Ticket type	Price
Adult	$44.95
Seniors (65 and up)	$39.95
Child (4 to 12 years old)	$34.95
Children 3 and under	Free
Three-course lunch (fresh catch of the day or vegetarian) (add-on)	$35
Ocean Aloha 32 oz. bottle	$62.95
Make tickets refundable	$3.50 per ticket

Visitor Admission and Behind the Scenes

Ticket type	Price
Adult	$69.90
Seniors (65 and up)	$64.90
Child (4 to 12 years old)	$59.90
Children 3 and under	Free
Three-course lunch (fresh catch of the day or vegetarian) (add-on)	$35
Ocean Aloha 32 oz. bottle	$62.95
Make tickets refundable	$3.50 per ticket

Visitor Admission and Plant Tour

Ticket type	Price
Adult	$79.90
Seniors (65 and up)	$74.90
Child (4 to 12 years old)	$69.90
Children 3 and under	Free
Three-course lunch (fresh catch of the day or vegetarian) (add-on)	$35
Ocean Aloha 32 oz. bottle	$62.95
Make tickets refundable	$3.50 per ticket

Military Admission Only

Military visitors must have a valid Military ID.

Ticket type	Price
Adult	$27.95
Seniors (65 and up)	$24.95
Child (4 to 12 years old)	$17.95
Children 3 and under	Free
Make tickets refundable	$3.50 per ticket

Military Admission and Behind-the-Scenes

Ticket type	Price
Adult	$52.90
Seniors (65 and up)	$49.90
Child (4 to 12 years old)	$42.90
Children 3 and under	Free
Make tickets refundable	$3.50 per ticket

Military Admission and Plant Tour

Ticket type	Price
Adult	$62.90
Seniors (65 and up)	$59.90
Child (4 to 12 years old)	$52.90
Children 3 and under	Free
Make tickets refundable	$3.50 per ticket

Shark Dive

For the shark dive experience, guests must be at least 13 years old, and you must have a scuba certification for open water or higher.

Tier type	What it includes	Price per person
Tier 1: Basic equipment	Weight and air tank	$350
Tier 2: Basic+ equipment	Weight, air tank, and regulator and buoyancy compensator device	$400
Tier 3: Basic++ equipment	Weight, air tank, regulator and buoyancy compensator device, wetsuit, gear rental mask, and fins	$450

Aquari-OM Tickets (Yoga)

Ticket type	Price
General admission (13 and up)	$30
Seniors (65 and up)	Free

Road to Hana

The Road to Hana is a beautiful scenic route that winds along the northeastern coast of Maui. This long stretch of highway is about 64 miles long, starting from the town of Kahului and ending in the small, remote community of Hana. Along this road, you will encounter several stunning waterfalls, panoramic views of ocean vistas, lush rainforests, and other roadside attractions. Here are some of the places worth checking out if you follow the Road to Hana:

- Garden of Eden at mile marker 10.5: The Garden of Eden is a tropical rainforest spanning 26 acres. This attraction shows its diverse collection of over 500 vibrant, colorful, and sometimes rare plant species. For film buffs, you may recognize this rainforest as it was featured in the opening of Spielberg's 1993 film Jurassic Park. The admission fee to visit the Garden of Eden is $20 for visitors who are 16 years old and up, $10 for those 5 to 15 years old, and free for those four and under. The park is open daily from 8 a.m. to 4 p.m.
- Honomanu Bay Lookout at mile marker 14: This is one the best places to stop along the Road to Hana as it offers unparalleled views of the highway winding along the cliffs. If you are stopping on the pull-off to take in the views from this spot, remember to exercise caution for passing vehicles.
- Keanae Peninsula and Village at mile marker 17: If you stop at the Keanae Peninsula and Village, you will be rewarded with fabulous coastal views of the peninsula, the Haleakala volcano, and its recent lava flows.

Iao Valley State Park

Address: 54 S High St, Wailuku, HI 96793

Hours of operation: 7 a.m. to 6 p.m. daily

Iao Valley State Park is a valley set within two deep-emerald-green peaks rich with history, and it is the home to the iconic Iao Needle, a towering volcanic rock about 1,200 feet above the valley's floor. This park was also the battleground for the famous 1790 Battle of the Kepaniwai, where King Kamehameha I battled against the army in Maui as he pushed forward to unite the chain of islands.

As you visit this state park, you'll explore the well-maintained trails that bring you through the lush rainforests and see native animals and birds. This is also an excellent spot to picnic and enjoy the surrounding area. If you visit the Kepaniwai Park Interpretive Center, you'll also learn more about the valley's history and the significance of the Battle of the Kepaniwai.

If you plan to visit on a day pass, the entrance fee per person is $5 (free for children 3 and under), and parking fees are $10.

Turtle Town

Turtle Town isn't exactly a town but a nickname for Maluaka Beach, where you can watch the Hawaiian Green Sea turtles in their natural habitat. This is a remarkable experience because these are some of the gentlest turtles in the world—and sometimes curious! If you're swimming and do it slowly, they'll swim beside you. You may never get to do this elsewhere in the world, so I highly recommend going to Maluka Beach if you're going to be in Maui.

You can access the beach by land, but keep in mind that coral reefs protect it, so taking a guided kayak tour is recommended. Maui Kayak Adventures is a great one to check out as their tour groups are small, so you can chat more with your tour guide and get as close as possible to the wildlife.

The Island of Maui Beaches

Makena Beach

Makena Beach, also known as "Big Beach," has a beautiful setting with golden sand. This beach is about two-thirds of a mile long and has clear waters perfect for snorkeling and exploring the fish in the sea. The surf is also gentle if you're learning to surf or bodyboard. There are also lifeguards on duty, bathrooms, and short hikes nearby.

Napili Bay Beach

Napili Bay Beach is on the northwest coast of Maui. This white sandy beach has crystal clear waters, gentle waves, and perfect swimming, surfing, and snorkeling opportunities. This beach does not have a lifeguard on duty.

Ka'anapali Beach

Ka'anapali Beach is well-known for its beautiful scenery, clear waters, and golden sand. Visitors of this beach enjoy snorkeling in the water to explore the coral reefs and the diverse marine life within its waters. A lifeguard is on duty at this beach between 8 a.m. and 4 p.m.

What NOT To Do - Hawaii

Hamoa Beach

Hamoa Beach is on Maui's eastern coast in Hana and is a favored destination for visitors and locals thanks to its natural beauty and stunning surroundings. This beach is tucked within some cliffs with lush tropical foliage. The beach has gentle waves, which is ideal for people who are not strong swimmers or have little ones.

Palauea "White Rocks" Beach

Palauea Beach, known as "White Rocks" Beach, is a little south of the Kea Lani Beach Hotel. This beach offers a place to relax, laze in the sun, snorkel, and scuba dive to explore the fish and other marine life in the crystal-clear waters.

What Events to Enjoy on the Island of Maui

Olukai Hoʻolauleʻa

The Olukai Hoʻolauleʻ is an annual sports festival and cultural celebration every May on the north shores of the island. This event brings top athletes from around the world to compete in the open ocean and stand-up paddleboard races. Additionally, this event aims to honor and celebrate Hawaiian culture, community, and connection to the sea with other family-friendly activities.

East Maui Taro Festival

Address: 200 S. High St, Kalana O Maui Bldg, Wailuku, HI 96793

The East Maui Taro Festival is held in Hāna every April. This event has significant Hawaiian cultural significance, celebrating the taro (or kalo in Hawaiian), a staple plant in traditional Hawaiian cuisine.

You can find live music, arts and crafts, a farmer's market, and plenty of food tents with their take on a taro dish during this event. This festival is a free event and takes place at the Hanna Ballpark.

Kapalua Wine and Food Festival

The Kapalua Wine and Food Festival is an annual event held at the Kapalua Resort every June. This festival features a series of culinary experiences, including wine tastings led by sommeliers, cooking demonstrations, food and wine pairings, and delicious meals prepared by renowned chefs. Tickets start from around $150 to over $1,200 (if you want to attend all the events over the three days).

Hawaiian Slack-Key Guitar Festival

The Hawaiian Slack-Key Guitar Festival occurs annually in October to celebrate the traditional Hawaiian music style of slack-key guitar. This unique musical event involves musicians fingerpicking guitars with loosened strings to produce a different sound.

Maui Film Festival

The Maui Film Festival takes place annually at the Grand Wailea Resort, showcasing films from around the globe. The festival happens over a few days, screening movies under the stars at outdoor venues for an immersive viewing experience against Maui's beautiful landscape. In addition to film screenings, there are special events you can attend, including panel discussions, filmmaker Q&As, and an award ceremony to honor the outstanding films.

Where to Eat on the Island of Maui

Café o'Lei at the Mill House

Address: 1670 Honoapiilani Hwy, Wailuku, HI 96793

Hours of operation

- Tuesday to Friday: 11 a.m. to 8 p.m.
- Saturday and Sunday: 9 a.m. to 8 p.m.

Café o'Lei at the Mill House offers some stunning sites as you enjoy your meal with the jagged West Maui Mountains in the distance. This restaurant is a part of the Maui Tropical Plantation and has some neat nods to Maui's plantation heritage, including giant mill gears and two steam engines. You can expect some delicious meals, including lamb shank and polenta; however, if you're seeking a quick happy hour drink when their cocktail menu is cheap.

Ichiban Okazuya

Address: 2133 Kaohu St, Wailuku, HI 96793

Hours of operation: 10 a.m. to 7 p.m., Monday to Friday

Ichiban Okazuya is a Japanese restaurant that will satisfy anyone's taste buds! This restaurant is family-owned and quick to get your meals ready. Some favorite dishes include their vegetable tempura, Korean chicken, and chow fun.

Hula Grill Kaanapali

Address: 2435 Kaanapali Pkwy, Bldg. P1, Lahaina, HI 96761

Hours of operation

- Brunch: Saturdays and Sundays between 10 a.m. and 2 p.m.
- Lunch: 11 a.m. to 4 p.m. daily.
- Barefoot bar: 4 p.m. to 9:30 p.m. daily
- Dinner: 4:30 p.m. to 9:30 p.m. daily

The Hula Grill Kaanapali is one of the iconic restaurants in Maui with a 1930s beach house vibe. All tables view the ocean and the neighboring islands of Lanai and Molokai. This restaurant is known for its commitment to using fresh, locally sourced ingredients in its diverse menu, which includes seafood and grilled meats. If you come here in the evening, you will enjoy traditional Hawaiian entertainment as they have live music between 5:30 p.m. and 8 p.m. daily and a hula show from 6:30 p.m. to 7:30 p.m.

Esters Fair Prospect

Address: 2050 Main St, STE 1B, Wailuku, HI 96793

Hours of operation

- Monday, Tuesday, and Saturday: 3 p.m. to 12 a.m.
- Wednesday to Friday: 12 p.m. to 12 a.m.
- Closed on Sunday

Esters Fair Prospect is a cocktail lounge in Wailuku. This bar has a beautiful outdoor terrace where you can enjoy delicious cocktails as you take in the surrounding scenery of the IAO Valley. In addition to cocktails, you can enjoy a selection of appetizers made with locally sourced ingredients.

Tight Tacos Maui

Address: 349 Hanakai St B, Kahului, HI 96732

Hours of operation: 10 a.m. to 3 p.m. daily

Reggie Ballesteros opened Tight Tacos Maui, which is a popular place to go if you enjoy eating tacos! When the restaurant opens, people are lining up to get their meals. Some of the most popular menu items include the rajas in freshly pressed tortillas and carnitas, which burst with flavor. For a budget-friendly date, check out this establishment on Taco Tuesdays, when you can get tacos for $3!

Kitoko Maui

Address: Piikea Ave, Kihei, HI 96753

Hours of operation
- Tuesday to Saturday from 11:30 a.m. to 8 p.m.
- Sunday: 8 a.m. to 2 p.m.

If you're in the mood for a five-star meal without breaking the bank, visit the Kitoko Maui food truck. This food truck is steps away from Laie Beach and offers a diverse range of bento boxes bursting with flavor!

Tin Roof

Address: 360 Papa Pl, Kahului, HI 96732

Hours of operation: Tuesday to Saturday from 10 a.m. to 8 p.m.

Fans of the TV show Top Chef are in for a treat if you go to Tin Roof! This restaurant was founded by Top Chef alum Sheldon Simeon, who serves meals reflecting Hawaii's rich cuisine. You can customize your bowls with your choice of white or brown rice, kale, or the most popular option, garlic noodles, topped with garlic shrimp, steak, poke, fried chicken, or pork belly. In addition to bowls, you can order sandwiches, salads, or other noodle-based dishes.

Spago

Address: 3900 Wailea Alanui Dr, Kihei, HI 96753

Hours of operation: 5 p.m. to 9 p.m.

Spago is a great restaurant option for a lovely evening out. This establishment is in the Four Seasons Maui Resort in Wailea and offers a menu inspired by Hawaiian flavors and made with top ingredients.

Ferraro's Bar e Ristorante

Address: 3900 Wailea Alanui Dr, Kihei, HI 96753

Hours of operation: 11 a.m. to 9 p.m.

If you're looking for another option at the Four Seasons Maui Resort, check out Ferraro's Bar e Ristorante, which offers lunch and dinner menu options with stunning views of the Pacific Ocean. The menu at this restaurant has an exciting twist on Italian dishes and delivers meals for those who are vegetarian or vegan.

Paia Fish Market

Address: 100 Hana Hwy, Paia, HI 96779

Hours of operation: 11 a.m. to 9 p.m. daily

Paia Fish Market is a popular spot on the corner of Hana Highway and Baldwin Avenue in Paia Town. This establishment offers a relaxed dining atmosphere with picnic-style seating and budget-friendly prices on their food options, which is great if you're in Maui with your family. Some hit menu options include fish burgers, French fries, and coleslaw.

What to Eat on the Island of Maui

Lilikoi Butter

Lilikoi, or passion fruit, is a tropical fruit native to Hawaii that's known for its sweet and tangy flavor. Lilikoi butter is made by combining lilikoi juice with butter and sugar, resulting in a delicious spread that's perfect for topping toast or pancakes.

Taro Pancakes

Taro pancakes are a unique twist on traditional pancakes, made with taro flour or mashed taro root for a subtly sweet and earthy flavor. They're often served with coconut syrup or lilikoi (passion fruit) butter for an extra burst of tropical flavor.

Fish Tacos

Maui is known for its fresh seafood, and fish tacos are a popular dish that showcases the island's flavors. Grilled or blackened fish is served in soft tortillas and topped with cabbage slaw, salsa, and creamy sauces for a flavorful and satisfying meal.

Butter Coconut Mochi

Mochi is a Japanese rice cake made from glutinous rice that's pounded into a paste and molded into various shapes. In Maui, you'll find mochi filled with coconut cream, making them a delightful snack or dessert option.

Where to Stay on the Island of Maui

One thing to note about staying in Maui and looking at accommodations is that most will be in the mid-to-higher range. If you seek something that won't break the bank, remember to check out Airbnb and Vrbo listings!

Polynesian Shores 118

Address: Kahana, 96761

Polynesian Shores is a self-catering option on a condo's ground floor with a stunning ocean view. This condo has an outdoor pool, a hot tub, a barbecue area, and a private beach.

Aston Kaanapali Shores

Address: 3445 Honoapiilani Rd, Lahaina, HI 96761

The Aston Kaanapali Shores Hotel is located along the shores of Kaanapali Beach and features an ocean-front pool and ocean-view rooms. This luxury hotel offers many spa amenities, including a hot tub, sauna, and other treatments. If you are curious about scuba diving, complimentary lessons at this hotel are worth taking advantage of! For other ways to immerse yourself in Hawaiian experiences, you can join in on a ukulele class.

Banana Bungalow Maui Hostel

Address: 310 N Market St, Wailuku, HI 96793

If you happen to be traveling to Hawaii for a solo adventure, check out the Banana Bungalow Maui Hostel. This hostel is an affordable and laid-back accommodation, providing you with a welcoming and communal atmosphere where you can mingle with other travelers. At this hostel, you will find dormitory-style rooms with shared facilities. It's also conveniently located near beaches, hiking trails, and some of Maui's cultural sites.

The Mauian Hotel

Address: 5441 Lower Honoapiilani Rd, Lahaina, HI 96761

If you're looking for a charming and laid-back retreat in Maui, the Mauian Hotel is an excellent accommodation. The rooms feature a contemporary look with bamboo mat ceilings, private shower-only bathrooms, mini-fridges, and microwaves. If you choose a studio-sized room, you'll find a full kitchen to suit your needs. However, neither the rooms nor studios have a TV or telephone—you can find these in the spacious family lounge area where a continental breakfast is served. Additional amenities include a pool and barbecues. They also have a poolside party with live entertainment.

This hotel has no resort fees, and parking is free if you have rented a car.

Sands of Kahana

Address: 4299 L. Honoapiilani Rd, Lahaina, HI 96761

Sands of Kahana is a large condo that offers comfortable accommodations. The property is surrounded by lush gardens, and some apartments overlook the Pacific Ocean. All rooms have a fully equipped kitchen, outdoor pool, barbecues, and gym.

Hale Hui Kai

Address: 2994 South Kihei Rd, Kihei, HI 96753

Hale Hui Kai is a great, affordable option for families who want a comfortable and convenient stay during their time in Hawaii. This condo has plenty of spacious units just steps from Keawakapu Beach. All units have fully equipped kitchens to allow flexibility when preparing meals. Also, guests can swim in their oceanfront pool or watch whales from their private balconies. This accommodation is a short drive from various attractions in Maui and the Wailea and Makena golf courses.

The Banyan Bed and Breakfast

Address: 3265 Baldwin Ave, Makawao, HI 96768

The Banyan Bed and Breakfast is a lovely accommodation in the Upcountry of Maui atop the slopes of Haleakalā. This property has beautiful rooms decorated with traditional Hawaiian decor and is fitted with modern amenities. In addition to breakfast served every morning, guests can use the barbecue on the property, enjoy their saltwater pool, and sit in their gardens.

Kula Lodge

Address: 15200 Haleakala Hwy, Kula, HI 96790

Kula Lodge is situated atop the slopes of Haleakalā and features five lodges for a tranquil retreat. At this accommodation, each has its Maui-rustic look, complete with wooden ceilings and picturesque views of the surrounding lush tropical area. This accommodation also has an excellent restaurant on-site offering delicious, hearty comfort meals. Some nearby attractions of the Kula Lodge include hiking trails in the Haleakalā National Park.

Maui Ocean Breezes

Address: 760 S Kihei Rd #107, Kihei, HI 96753

Maui Ocean Breezes is a more remote option while on the island of Maui. This eco-friendly accommodation is family-owned, and its rooms will leave you calm and centered. Each room has a partly or wholly equipped kitchen and a private balcony. Additional amenities include a pool and a meditation hut facing the ocean.

Four Seasons Resort Maui at Wailea

Address: 3900 Wailea Alanui Dr, Kihei, HI 96753

If you want to splurge, staying at the Four Seasons Resort Maui will offer an amazing tropical paradise experience for your vacation. This resort is along the beautiful shores of Wailea Beach, with some rooms overlooking the Pacific Ocean. This resort has three pools, including an infinity pool for adults and a family-friendly one with a water slide. Additionally, there are spa services, a golf course, and several dining options (including the two we explored earlier in this chapter).

What Not to Do on the Island of Maui

Don't Go to Maui Souvenir Shops

It is always tempting to go to souvenir shops on a trip. However, if you're looking for something authentic, the chances of finding something in a generic souvenir store are not the place to go. (Plus, they'll lure you in with "free with purchase" promotions.) If you want to bring home authentic gifts, check out the Maui Ocean Treasures shop in the Maui Ocean Center Aquarium or the Maui Swap Meet shop in Kahului.

Check Educational Programs at Maui Ocean Center

Take advantage of educational programs and talks offered by the aquarium to learn more about marine life conservation and protection. Also, it's advisable to use audio guides or informational signage to enhance your understanding of the exhibits and marine life. Refrain from using flash photography as it can startle or stress marine animals and disrupt their natural behaviors. Please note that food and drink are not allowed outside the aquarium to maintain cleanliness and prevent contamination of the exhibits.

Drive Safe while on the Road to Hana

The Road to Hana is winding and narrow, with many hairpin turns and blind corners. Slow down and drive cautiously to avoid accidents and enjoy the scenery. Avoid driving the Road to Hana at night, as visibility is limited and there are few streetlights along the route. Ensure your vehicle is in good condition and has a full tank of gas before embarking on the trip. Bring plenty of water, snacks, and sunscreen for the journey. Plan to spend a full day on the Road to Hana to allow time for stops and exploration along the way. Rushing through the journey can detract from the experience. Many roadside stands and attractions along the Road to Hana only accept cash, so be sure to bring enough money with you. Take breaks at designated rest areas to stretch your legs, use the restroom, and enjoy the scenery.

Don't Eat at Chain Restaurants

Chain restaurants may be convenient, but they don't all offer authentic Hawaiian cuisine (and sometimes they are overpriced). Instead, go where the locals enjoy dining out! You'll find some great authentic options and a completely different vibe!

Don't Take Surfing Lessons with Big Surf School Companies

If learning to surf in Hawaii is on your bucket list, all the power to you! But avoid taking lessons with a big Maui surf school company. There will be a large class and not enough instructors to help you master the sport due to the rushed nature. Consider a private company offering surfing lessons if you can allot the budget. You'll get a one-on-one approach, and you're guaranteed to ride a wave!

Don't Take a Discounted Boat Tour

Discounts are great, especially when you're vacationing. However, avoid the cheap ones when experiencing a boat tour. Chances are, you will be squished like a sardine on a boat with little room to see, especially if you intend to go whale spotting. Instead, look for boat companies that take a small number of people. It may be a little more expensive, but the service and the ability to see will be better!

Don't Forget to Research the Areas Affected by the Wildfires

In August 2023, Maui experienced one of its most devastating wildfires that swept through parts of the island. However, Lanai and West Maui were the two most affected, as well as some of the Upcountry areas. Be sure to research some places you intend to visit before visiting.

Be careful with Turtles at Turtle Village.

Maintain a respectful distance from turtles while observing them in their natural habitat. It is recommended to stay at least 10 feet away. Avoid touching or disturbing sea turtles, as they are protected by law and can be easily stressed by human interaction. Refrain from feeding sea turtles, as it can disrupt their natural feeding behaviors and may be harmful to their health.

Next Stop: The Island of Molokai

The Island of Maui is stunning, filled with adventure and relaxation, so you can make your vacation whatever you want! This chapter taught you about some attractions, including the Haleakalā National Park, Maui Ocean Center, and the top beaches to laze about in the sun.

In the next chapter, we will be island hopping to Molokai to explore all of the things you can do on this Hawaiian island.

Chapter 5:

Molokai Island —Dos and Don'ts

O f all the islands in Hawaii, Molokai is the most laid back and maintains much of Hawaii's ancient traditions and customs. It's also one of the islands believed to be the birthplace of the traditional hula dance. Though Big Island and Maui also claim to be where this traditional dance originated, its origins are a bit murky. However, when you visit this island, you can expect some of the most authentic Hawaiian experiences because they, surprisingly, resist as much traditional tourism as possible.

Discovering the Island of Molokai

Molokai is the fifth-largest Hawaiian island and is home to 8,000 people, most of whom are native Hawaiians. This beautiful island is one of the best-kept secrets and has a culture still deeply rooted in Hawaiian traditions, making for an authentic Hawaiian experience.

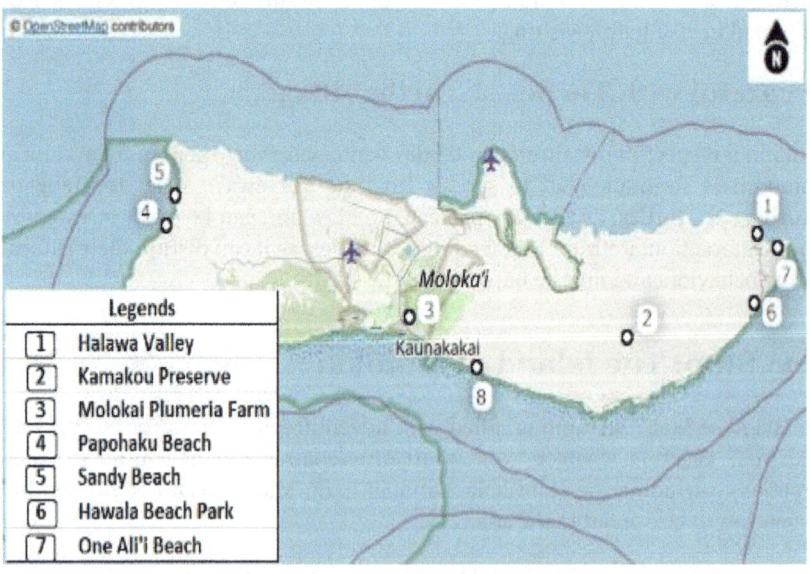

What NOT To Do - Hawaii

Like the other Hawaiian Islands, Molokai was formed by two volcanoes: Wailau and Mauna Loa. These volcanoes made for some stunning geography with towering sea cliffs and stunning white beaches. Additionally, it has the longest coral reef throughout the archipelago, allowing marine life to flourish.

In addition to its nonbusy lifestyle and beautiful scenery, this island has seen its fair share of history, including the former leper colony where Father Damien dedicated his life to helping those who were infected.

The allure of the quieter lifestyle makes for a great adventure, especially if you want to spend a week here. Let's dive right into the things to do on the island of Molokai.

What to Do on the Island of Molokai

Halawa Valley Cultural Hike

Address: There is no set address for this attraction. However, to get there, you will need to follow the Kamehameha Highway, heading east for about 26 miles.

Hours of operation: Tours occur on Mondays, Tuesdays, Thursdays, Fridays, and Saturdays between 9 a.m. and 2:30 p.m. unless their calendar specifies otherwise.

The Halawa Valley Cultural Hike is one of the most special excursions you can take on the island of Molokai. This is more than just a 3.4-mile hike—it's an experience that will bring you to a deeper understanding of Hawaiian culture and heritage. The Halawa Valley is a private property owned by those who live here. Interestingly, this part of Molokai has been home to many Hawaiians since 650!

Before you begin your hike, you will learn about the history of the owners' families and how they preserve their traditions and customs. You'll see a traditional greeting and even partake in it if you're comfortable. You'll also learn about the 1946 tsunami and see photos of its devastation on the island.

On the hike, your guide will take you to the waterfall. Along the way, you'll learn about the different plant species, see historic sites, and hear the stories that have passed through the generations. If the weather is nice, you can swim at Moa'ula Falls.

For this hike, you must wear comfortable closed-toe shoes or hiking boots. The hike difficulty is intermediate to advanced. If you intend to swim, wear your swimsuit under your hiking clothes and ensure you have a dry towel in your backpack.

Ticket type	Price
Adult: culture and waterfall	$75
Adult: culture only	$45
Child: culture and waterfall (4 years old to 12 years old)	$45
Child: culture only (4 years old to 12 years old)	$25
Child under 4 (all excursions)	Free

Should you need to cancel, you must do so at least 48 hours in advance. If you cancel with less notice than that, you will not receive a refund. However, you will receive a full refund if the tour needs to be canceled due to adverse weather.

Kamakou Preserve

The Kamakou Preserve is a protected rainforest encompassing about 2,774 acres of land on the slopes of Mount Kamakou, the highest peak on the island of Molokai. This preserve is home to many native Hawaiian plants and animals, many rare or endangered. The Nature Conservancy oversees the preserve and offers monthly hikes between April and October. To visit Kamakou, you will need a four-wheel drive vehicle to get there. You'll also want to ensure you are wearing the appropriate clothing. There is also no cell service in the mountains.

Soaring Sea Cliffs

Molokai has some of the most impressive sea cliffs—but you can't see them because no roads lead you there. So, if you want to see these cliffs, you'll want to take a helicopter ride from Maui, or if you're traveling to Molokai for a few days while on your vacation, book your flight from Maui to Molokai. Some of the helicopter tour options are

- Sunshine Helicopters
- Blue Hawaiian Helicopters
- Pacific Helicopters
- Air Maui Helicopters

Prices for these tours start around $250 and can go up to about $400 for a 45-minute to 50-minute tour.

Molokai Plumeria Farm

Address: 1342 Maunaloa Hwy, Kaunakakai, HI 96748

Molokai Plumeria Farm is worth visiting if you're looking for a fun day with your family. Plumeria is one of Hawaii's iconic flowers used in their leis. At the farm, you can take a tour and learn about the history of the flowers, then learn how to make your own lei.

Tours take place from 9 a.m. to 10 a.m. and are $40 per person. This can be scheduled between Monday and Friday.

The Island of Molokai's Beaches

Papohaku Beach Park

Papohaku Beach Park is along the west coast side of Molokai and is the biggest beach on this Hawaiian Island. This beach is three miles long, has beautiful soft white sand, and is a great place to visit if you're looking to enjoy the scenery. Unlike some other beaches on Molokai, this one remains relatively uncrowded, so you won't have to worry too much about finding a place to set up and bask in the sun. Papohaku Beach Park is also an excellent beach to visit if you want to watch a stunning sunset.

While the waters are mostly clear, it's not recommended to swim as the currents can be strong, and there are coral reefs you can hurt yourself on if you're not careful.

Kepuhi Beach

Kepuhi Beach is another beach that is rarely crowded, which makes for a great, peaceful beach day, especially if you bring a book. This beach also has a long stretch of white sand with palm trees on one end. While this beach is often deserted, it's not a great swimming beach due to the rough waters.

What NOT To Do - Hawaii

Sandy Beach

If you are seeking a beach that is great for swimming, snorkeling, or body surfing, you will want to check out Sandy Beach. What's lovely about this beach is that the ocean floor is deep, so you can enter the water without any worries about stepping on sharp rocks or coral reefs.

Halawa Beach Park

Halawa Beach Park is a popular option if you're looking for a great beach to fish, bask in the sun, or picnic. This beach park has two different beaches: Kawili Beach on the east and Kama'alaea Beach on the west. The waters here are generally shallow unless the surf is up; however, they're also murky, making snorkeling challenging. Plus, you may be less inclined to swim if you can't see what lurks in the waters.

While here, explore the picturesque Halawa Valley, where you can view the waterfall and utilize the picnic area, barbecues, and bathroom.

One Ali'i Beach Park

One Ali'i Beach Park is the most popular beach on the island of Molokai. This beach is located near Kaunakakai and has plenty of things to do, including camping, fishing, and watching the sunset. If you intend to spend the day at the beach, the water is often murky, so it doesn't make for great swimming or snorkeling—it is great for dipping your feet in, though!

Where to Eat on the Island of Molokai

Molokai Burger

Address: 20 W Kamehameha V Hwy, Kaunakakai, HI 96748

Hours of operation: 7 a.m. to 9 p.m. daily

Molokai Burger is a popular eatery known for its diverse menu options and quick service. This restaurant offers a breakfast menu, an extensive burger menu, and a healthy menu to suit anyone's taste buds. The prices are great, too, for those sticking to a tighter budget.

Paddlers Restaurant and Bar

Address: 10 Mohala St, Kaunakakai, HI 96748

Hours of operation: 11 a.m. to 8 p.m., Tuesday to Saturday.

Paddlers Restaurant and Bar is a fancier place to dine out at, which is shocking given its laid-back atmosphere. You can expect a diverse menu from American-style to Hawaiian dishes at this establishment. Prices for this place are low to mid-range, depending on what you choose to eat.

Molokai Pizza Cafe

Address: 15 Kaunakakai Pl, Kaunakakai, HI 96748

Hours of operation

- Monday to Friday: 10 a.m. to 10 p.m.
- Saturday and Sunday: 10 a.m. to 11 p.m.

Who doesn't love pizza, especially if you can grab one from the Molokai Pizza Cafe? This pizza joint serves various pizzas, each made with locally sourced ingredients. In addition to pizza, they also have pasta dishes, ribs, chicken, salads, and a kid's menu.

Kanemitsu's Bakery and Coffee Shop

Address: 79 Ala Malama Ave, Kaunakakai, HI 96748

Hours of operation: 5:30 a.m. to 5 p.m., Wednesday to Sunday

If you're looking for a simple way to start your day or grab a quick lunch, check out Kanemitsu's Bakery and Coffee Shop. This establishment has been around since the 1920s and is well-loved for its breakfast and freshly baked bread (perfect if you stay at a self-catering accommodation).

Manae Goods and Grindz

Address: 615 Kamehameha V Hwy, Kaunakakai, HI 96748

Hours of operation: 8 a.m. to 3:30 p.m. daily

Manae Goods and Grindz is a beloved establishment among the Molokai locals. You will find a great menu at this restaurant serving authentic Hawaiian cuisine, from teri beef to loco moco and much more! They also have a breakfast menu if you are seeking breakfast options while on Molokai. All the prices are relatively cheap, too!

Ono Fish & Shrimp Truck

Address: 53 Ala Malama Ave, Kaunakakai, HI 96748

Hours of operation: Monday to Friday from 11 a.m. to 2:30 p.m.

If you love seafood, you'll love the Ono Fish & Shrimp Truck menu! This food truck serves up plenty of delicious fish and shellfish options. People rave about their fish and shrimp tacos if that's something you enjoy.

Hula Bean Cafe

Address: 35 Mohala St #6, Kaunakakai, HI 96748

Hours of operation

- Monday to Saturday: 6:30 a.m. to 5 p.m.
- Sunday: 8 a.m. to 5 p.m.

If you're looking to start your day early and want to grab a quick bite on the way, go visit Hula Bean Cafe to get your coffee and breakfast. This cafe serves a wide range of coffee and espresso drinks, breakfast sandwiches, smoothies, and paninis. The prices are also cheap, making it great for keeping to a stricter travel budget.

A Taste of Moloka'i

Address: 82A Ala Malama Ave, Kaunakakai, HI 96748

Hours of operation

- Monday to Friday: 10 a.m. to 4:30 p.m.
- Saturday: 8:30 a.m. to 2:30 p.m.

A Taste of Molokai is a food truck stop that serves poke, acai bowls, and salads. This is a great spot to pick up lunch and enjoy it on the beach if you want something lighter or healthier. The poke salad is one of the popular choices on their menu, as people love the flavor and texture of everything together. They also have a cheap breakfast menu option!

Big Daddy's Store and Restaurant

Address: 67 Ala Malama Ave, Kaunakakai, HI 96748

Hours of operation: 9 a.m. to 5 p.m. daily

Big Daddy's Store and Restaurant is great for authentic Filipino dishes. It may look like a hole-in-the-wall establishment, but its delicious food has a great kick. Prices are also relatively cheap.

What to Eat on the Island of Molokai

Manapua

Manapua is a Hawaiian adaptation of the Chinese baozi, or steamed bun, filled with savory fillings such as char siu pork, chicken, or vegetables. It's a popular snack or meal option that's perfect for enjoying on the go. Manapua can be found at local bakeries, food trucks, and markets throughout Molokai.

Pipikaula

Pipikaula is a traditional Hawaiian dish made from seasoned and dried strips of beef, similar to beef jerky. The beef is typically marinated in a mixture of soy sauce, garlic, and other seasonings before being dried or smoked. Pipikaula is a delicious and portable snack that's perfect for enjoying while exploring the island.

Kūlolo

Kūlolo is a traditional Hawaiian dessert made from taro and coconut. It's a sweet and dense pudding-like dish that's typically steamed in ti leaves, giving it a unique flavor and aroma. Kūlolo is often enjoyed as a dessert or snack and is a delicious way to experience traditional Hawaiian flavors.

Mochiko Chicken

Mochiko chicken is a popular Hawaiian dish made with bite-sized pieces of chicken marinated in a mixture of soy sauce, sugar, garlic, and ginger, then coated in sweet rice flour (mochiko) and fried until crispy and golden brown. It's a flavorful and addictive dish that's often served as an appetizer or main course.

Squid Luau

Squid luau is a classic Hawaiian dish made with tender pieces of squid cooked in creamy coconut milk and taro leaf sauce. The combination of flavors is rich and savory, with the sweetness of the coconut milk complementing the earthiness of the taro leaves. Squid luau is a popular dish at lū'au feasts and local gatherings.

Where to Stay on the Island of Molokai

Compared to some of the other Hawaiian Islands, there aren't many resort or hotel options on the island of Molokai. Your best option for staying on this island is to seek out Airbnbs. Otherwise, these self-catering options may work well, too.

Molokai Island Retreat

Address: 7146 Kamehameha V Hwy, Kaunakakai, HI 96748
Molokai Island Retreat is a condo on the island's east side at the Wavecrest Resort. You can use an oceanfront pool, a covered cabana, and barbecues at the resort. If you choose to stay here, Murphy's Beach is a short walk down the road, and there is a small grocery store three miles away.

What NOT To Do - Hawaii

Hotel Moloka'i

Address: 1300 Kamehameha V Hwy, Kaunakakai, HI 96748
Hotel Moloka'i is one of the few self-catering options on the island. This accommodation is along Kamiloloa Beach and has a unique design as it was built to model what a traditional Polynesian village would look like. Some of the rooms overlook the ocean, while others have views of the garden. If you stay here, your room will have a fridge, microwave, and a coffee maker. There is also a restaurant on site called Hiro's Ohana Grill, which is open between 11 a.m. and 9 p.m. If you want to snorkel at the beach, you can rent the equipment from the hotel.

Paniolo Hale

Address: 100 Lio Pl, Maunaloa, HI 96770
Paniolo Hale is along Kepuhi Beach and boasts excellent views of the ocean. This apartment has a fully equipped kitchen, and some rooms have a balcony. Guests are welcome to use the barbecue on-site and the swimming pool.

Molokai Shores

Address: Star Route, 1000 Kamehameha V Hwy, Kaunakakai, HI 96748
At Molokai Shores, you'll have an entire apartment to yourself that comes with a fully-equipped kitchen for your needs. This accommodation also has excellent ocean or garden views, a barbecue, and an outdoor swimming pool.

Pu'u O Hōkū Ranch

Address: Mm 25, Kaunakakai, HI 96748
If you want a more rustic retreat, check out Pu'u O Hōkū Ranch. This is a family-owned retreat, ranch, and farm on Molokai's east side. This is a great spot to stay if you're looking for outdoor activities or want to see how a working ranch goes about its days. As this place is for relaxation and unwinding, their cottages have no Wi-Fi. However, you can access it in their main lodge.

What Not to Expect on the Island of Molokai

Don't Expect a Luxury Vacation

As you have probably figured out by now, Molokai is one island that tends to keep to itself and doesn't have many tourist attractions. This is a good thing because the attractions won't be too busy. On the other hand, if you're looking for luxury options, you're also not going to find them on Molokai. Most of the accommodation options will be self-catering.

Don't Expect Partying and Nightlife

Molokai is a laid-back island, so people live simpler lives. If you're hoping to embrace a fun night out, chances are you won't get that here, as most things close down early!

Don't Expect to Be Entertained

Molokai doesn't have many tourist attractions, such as surfing lessons or other ways to fill your trip with activities. One of the benefits of visiting this Hawaiian Island is that it leaves you to decide what your days will look like. You've been given a few great options; however, you must be creative depending on how long you'll be on this island.

Obtain Necessary Permits before entering Kamakou Preserve.

Make sure to obtain any necessary permits or permissions before entering the Kamakou Preserve to ensure compliance with regulations and respect for the environment. Show respect for the cultural significance of the Kamakou Preserve by learning about its history and significance to the native Hawaiian people. Take advantage of interpretive signs, guided tours, and educational programs offered within the preserve to learn more about its unique ecosystems and conservation efforts. Be respectful of cultural artifacts and archaeological sites within the preserve, and avoid disturbing or removing any items.

Be Mindful of Farming Activities at Plumeria Farm

Be mindful of ongoing farm activities and avoid disrupting the work of farm staff or interfering with agricultural operations. Stay within designated pathways and respect farm boundaries to avoid trampling crops or entering restricted areas. If purchasing products from the farm, do so responsibly and support sustainable agriculture practices.

Next Stop: The Island of Oahu

Molokai is a great Hawaiian Island to visit if you're looking for more of a retreat than days filled with activities. Exploring this Hawaiian Island is a great time to reflect on life and how simple it can be when you don't need to rush around.

In the next chapter, we will head over to the Island of Oahu, most famous for Pearl Harbor, and where the Dole Plantation is today.

ALOHA

Chapter 6:

Oahu Islands—Dos and Don'ts

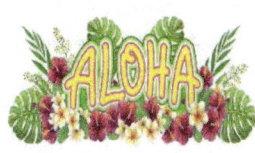

Duke Kahanamoku, often called the "Father of Modern Surfing," was a Hawaiian Olympic swimmer and a surfer whose influence helped shape the sport to where it is today. He earned multiple Olympic medals for the US in the 1912, 1920, and 1924 Summer Olympic Games, but it was surfing that he loved the most. He took his passion and began sharing the sport through a series of exhibitions and demonstrations for those to see, eventually helping the sport become more popular worldwide. If you're curious to see a statue of him, you can find it on the Waikiki Beach, often with leis hanging off his arms.

Discovering the Island of Oahu

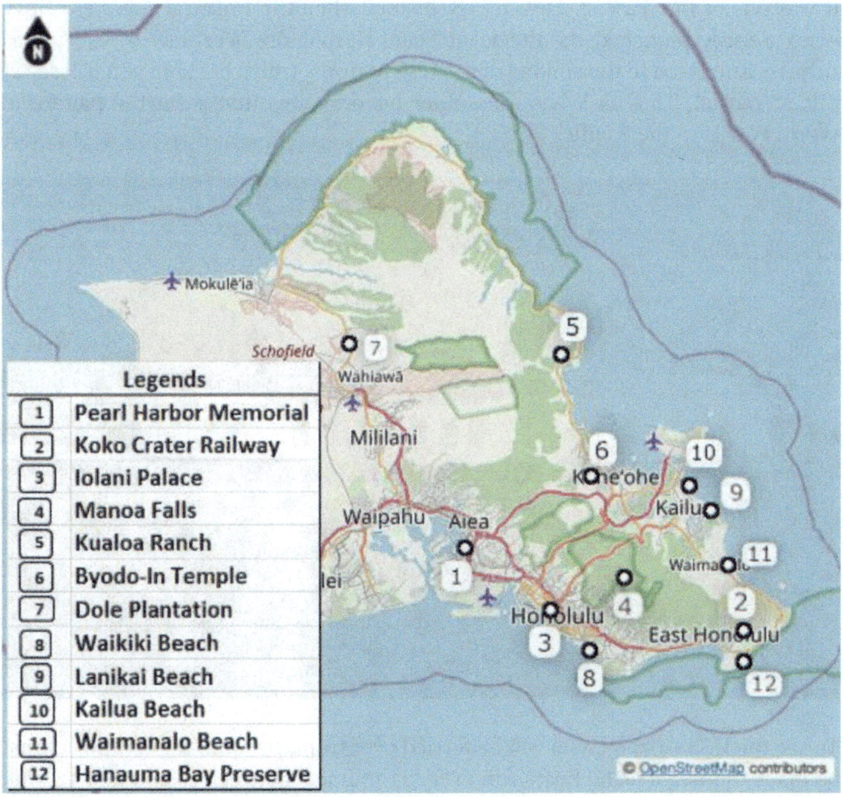
N
Mokulē'ia
Schofield
Wahiawā
Mililani
Waipahu
Aiea
Kāne'ohe
Kailua
Waimanalo
Honolulu
East Honolulu
Legends
1 Pearl Harbor Memorial
2 Koko Crater Railway
3 Iolani Palace
4 Manoa Falls
5 Kualoa Ranch
6 Byodo-In Temple
7 Dole Plantation
8 Waikiki Beach
9 Lanikai Beach
10 Kailua Beach
11 Waimanalo Beach
12 Hanauma Bay Preserve
© OpenStreetMap contributors

Oahu, often referred to as "The Gathering Place," is one of the liveliest islands of the Hawaiian Islands. This island is where most will spend their entire vacation (or at least a majority of it). While Honolulu is the state capital, there are plenty of other regions you can explore on this massive island. For the best surfing conditions, you'll want to go to the north shore; for pineapples, you'll go to the west, and in the center of the island are some of the largest attractions, including Pearl Harbor. Additionally, there are some excellent beaches on Oahu, including the famous Waikiki Beach. Whatever you decide to do on this island, you'll get a bit of history, a bit of adventure, and plenty of picturesque opportunities to incorporate into your vacation.

What to Do on the Island of Oahu

Pearl Harbor National Memorial

Address: 1 Arizona Memorial Pl, Honolulu, HI 96818

It was one of the darkest days in U.S. history when the Imperial Japanese Navy Army Service launched its attack on Pearl Harbor on December 7, 1941. This surprise attack led to the sinking of the USS Arizona, which is a ship you will see at this memorial. This park has nine other historic sites that paint the picture of World War II in the Pacific.

To see the USS Arizona, you will be ferried over from the land. Reservations must be made online, and the boats run every 15 minutes between 8 a.m. and 12 p.m.

and from 1 p.m. to 3:30 p.m. Reservations are $1 per person. If you are late, you'll be put on standby, so ensure you're not late! You also cannot change the time of your boat ticket. Additionally, there is a 23-minute documentary you can watch. However, it is not included with your ferry ticket, so plan extra time for this. There is no fee to see the other museums or the Pearl Harbor Visitor Center.

Koko Crater Railway Trail

Address: 7604 Koko Head Park Rd #7602, Honolulu, HI 96825

If you are up for a challenging hike that will reward you with beautiful scenery, check out the Koko Crater Railway Trail. This hike is 1.6 miles round-trip and will challenge you as you ascend an old military tramway from World War II that was used to transport soldiers and supplies. Along the way, looking into the area's history, you'll see some of the other remnants of the railway's past.

If you hike this, be prepared for a steep climb. There are 1,048 railroad ties plus another 30 feet to get to the lookout. Ensure you wear shoes with good tread, as the steps can be slippery from the dirt.

Iolani Palace

Address: 364 S King St, Honolulu, HI 96813

Iolani Palace is a significant historical site in Hawaii. This grand palace was constructed between 1879 and 1882 during the reign of King Kalakaua. It served as the royal residence of the Hawaiian monarchs under the Hawaiian Kingdom, which was overthrown a year later. This palace is renowned for its stunning architecture. It is the only recognized royal palace in the US. You can choose from several tours to gain a better insight into this historical fortress and its importance to Hawaii's history.

Audio Tours

On this self-guided tour, you will explore the first and second floors of the Iolani Palace alongside an audio guide that will dive into the palace's history, rooms, and furnishings. This tour should take no more than an hour, but you can go at your own pace.

Ticket type	Price
Adults (18 years old and up)	$26.95
Teens (13 to 17 years old)	$21.95
Children (5 to 12 years old)	$11.95
Children 4 and under	Free
Active military (18 years old and up with a valid ID)	$16.95
Military teens (13 to 17 years old)	$14.95
Military youth (5 to 12 years old)	$7.95

Docent-Led Tour

Take a tour with one of the Iolani Palace docents, who will take you back to the 19th century when the palace was completed. This tour will take you through the first and second floors as your guide tells you the history of the royal residents and their staterooms. The tour will conclude in the palace basement, where you can explore the exhibits at your own pace.

If you choose this tour option, ensure you arrive 30 minutes before your tour time.

Ticket type	Price
Adults (18 years old and up)	$32.95
Teens (13 to 17 years old)	$29.95
Children (5 to 12 years old)	$14.95
Children 4 and under	Free
Active military (18 years old and up with a valid ID)	$24.95
Military teens (13 to 17 years old)	$22.95
Military youth (5 to 12 years old)	$7.95

Chamberlain's Tour

During the Chamberlain's tour, you can tour the Chamberlain's office and other rooms not seen on the self-guided audio or docent-led tours. This is a unique experience as the groups are much smaller, allowing you the time to view some of the objects in the office and learn about the Royal Chamberlain's duties.

This tour is about 60 minutes and is limited to six people.

Ticket type	Price
Adults (13 years old and up)	$77.95
Children (5 to 12 years old)	$51.95

Fashion Fit for Royalty Tour

It is said the Hawaiian royals were some of the most well-dressed people in the islands. So, if you appreciate fashion, this will be a fun tour for you. You will get to see some of the contemporary pieces the Hawaiian royals wore and how they are significant in Hawaii's history. Additionally, you will get to see some of the staterooms, music room, and Chamberlain's office.

This tour is about 60 minutes and is limited to six people.

Ticket type	Price
Adults (18 years old and up)	$77.95
Children (5 to 13 years old)	$51.95

Manoa Falls

Manoa Falls is a much easier hike on Oahu Island. This trail is 1.6 a 1.6-mile-long round trip and will bring you through some lush rainforest, providing a serene and enchanting atmosphere toward the Mona Falls, a stunning 150-foot waterfall plunging into beautiful, sparkling waters below. This hike takes about two hours, depending on your fitness level. Remember to wear bug spray when hiking here because it can be buggy!

Kualoa Ranch Tours

Address: 49-560 Kamehameha Hwy, Kaneohe, HI 96744

Kualoa Ranch is a great attraction to go to if you're seeking all kinds of adventure. This ranch has several tours available, allowing you to see its expansive property and learn about some of the films filmed here, such as horseback riding, kayaking, and more!

Jurassic Valley Adventure Tour

Fans of Jurassic Park, Jurassic World, and Jurassic World: Fallen Kingdom will love this tour. You can join up to 15 other guests on this open-air bus that will take you around the ranch to see the filming locations and ancient fish ponds, rainforests, and waterfalls. This tour is about 2.5 hours long.

Ticket type	Price
Adult (13 years old and up)	$140
Children (3 to 12 years old)	$70

Jurassic Valley Ultra Terrain Vehicle Ride

Hop into an ultra terrain vehicle (UTV) and explore Kualoa's Ranch at your own pace (and on your adventure). These vehicles hold up to six people and can take you to some of the more remote areas of this stunning valley. Drivers must have a valid driver's license and be at least 21.

Ticket type	Price
Adult (13 years old and up)	$145
Children (5 to 12 years old)	$70

Hollywood Movie Sites Tour

On the Hollywood Movie Sites Tour, you'll take a 90-minute tour to see iconic filming locations from several films and TV shows.

What NOT To Do - Hawaii

Ticket type	Price
Adult (13 years old and up)	$52
Children (3 to 12 years old)	$37
Infant	Free

Jurassic Valley Zipline Adventure

The Jurassic Valley Zipline Adventure is more than just a ziplining experience; it also has some suspension bridges to cross and a short hike. This thrilling adventure will start at the top of the Ka'a'awa Valley and will have you zip-lining up to 200 feet. This experience is about three hours.

Ticket type	Price
Adult (13 years old and up)	$175
Children (10 to 12 years old)	$147

Horseback Ride Jurassic Valley

Take a nice horseback ride at the Kualoa Ranch. This two-hour adventure will take you through the valley, providing you with great views of the mountains and the opportunity to see different Jurassic Valley movie sites. Your guide will also give you some Hawaiian history on the ride.

Ticket type	Price
Adult (13 years old and up)	$145
Children (10 to 12 years old)	$90

Byodo-In Temple

Address: 47-200 Kahekili Hwy, Kaneohe, HI 96744

Hours of operation: 8:30 a.m. to 4:30 p.m. daily (the last admission is at 4:15 p.m.)

Byodo-In Temple is one of the most peaceful and serene places you can visit on the island of Oahu. This beautiful Buddhist temple in the Valley of Temples Memorial Park symbolizes peace, tranquility, and harmony. Interestingly, this temple is a smaller-scale replica modeled after the 900-year-old Byodo-In Temple in Uji, Japan. This temple commemorated the first Japanese immigrants who moved to Hawaii. You are welcome to explore the temple grounds, admire the Lotus Buddha, and partake in meditations. The calming atmosphere and stunning surroundings of the lush greenery and Ko'olau Mountains make it a popular destination for those seeking solace and spiritual rejuvenation.

Ticket type	Price
Adult (13 to 64 years old)	$5
Senior (65 and up)	$4
Child (2 to 12 years old)	$2
Children under 2	Free

Dole Plantation

Address: 64-1550 Kamehameha Hwy, Wahiawa, HI 96786

Hours of operation: 9:30 a.m. to 5:30 p.m. daily

At the Dole Plantation, you can view Hawaii's agricultural heritage and pineapple industry. There are several activities that will take you through the plantation to learn about the history of Dole and how it became the leading exporter of pineapples.

Pineapple Express Train Tour
On this train tour, you will be taken on a narrated journey through the plantation, learning stories about how the pineapple became Hawaii's influential crop and the

life of James Dole, who started the company and became the pioneer for exporting pineapples globally. This tour is about 2 miles long and lasts 20 minutes.

Ticket type	Price
Adults (13 years old and up)	$13.75
Children (4 to 12 years old)	$11.75
Children 3 and under	Free

Pineapple Garden Maze

Mazes are always fun, but the Pineapple Garden Maze has its accolades as it became known as the World's Largest Maze in the Guinness World Records in 2008. This maze, which has an intricate pineapple in the center, is a great way to test your navigation skills while searching for eight secret stations hidden throughout. If you're going to Hawaii with kids, this is a fun activity to do with your whole family!

Ticket type	Price
Adults (13 years old and up)	$9.25
Children (4 to 12 years old)	$7.25
Children 3 and under	Free

Plantation Garden Tour

The plantation garden tour will take you through eight mini gardens at Dole, allowing you to see, smell, and touch the crops being grown.

Ticket type	Price
Adults (13 years old and up)	$8
Children (4 to 12 years old)	$7.25
Children 3 and under	Free

Combo Tours

Ticket type	Train and garden	Train and maze	Maze and garden	Train, maze, and garden
Adults (13 years old and up)	$18.75	$19.75	$14	$27
Children (4 to 12 years old)	$15.25	$15.25	$11	$23
Children 3 and under	Free	Free	Free	Free

The Island of Oahu Beaches

Waikiki Beach

Waikiki Beach is the most famous beach in Hawaii, renowned for its stunning scenery and great views of the dormant Diamond Head volcano. This is an ideal destination for surfers and swimmers alike. The surf is excellent in the winter months. However, if you're in Honolulu in the summer, you'll find the waters calm, perfect for other outdoor water activities, including snorkeling and paddleboarding. This beach also has lifeguards and picnic areas during the day.

Lanikai Beach

Lanikai Beach is one of the island's most beautiful beaches on Oahu, with its powdery white sand and crystal clear turquoise waters. This beach is not as busy as other beaches on Oahu, allowing you the time to enjoy everything around it and just lay back. If you're up for a small hike, follow the Lanikai Pillbox Trail to see other great views of the beach and the surrounding islands. This beach does not have any additional amenities or a lifeguard.

Kailua Beach Park

If you plan your trip to Hawaii with your family, you will want to visit Kailua Beach Park. This beach is about 30 minutes from Honolulu and has a long stretch of white sand and flat waters, which makes it great for swimming, snorkeling, kayaking, or paddleboarding. There is a lifeguard at this beach, as well as bathrooms, showers, and a picnic area.

Waimanalo Beach

Waimanalo Beach is another excellent, family-friendly option for beach days. This beach boasts gorgeous white sand and crystal-clear waters with gentle waves that allow great swimming and other water activities, such as bodyboarding. If you plan to visit this beach on the weekend, try to get there early, as it can get busy.

Hanauma Bay Nature Preserve

If you're looking for other quieter beaches, the Hanauma Bay Nature Preserve is another great one. This beach is about a 30-minute drive from Honolulu and boasts picturesque scenery with crystal-clear turquoise waters framed by lush greenery. This beach is quieter in the mornings but can get busier as the day progresses, so be sure to visit in the morning if you want some tranquil time.

If you plan to visit Hanauma Bay Nature Preserve, there is an admission fee of $25 and a parking fee of $3. This beach is open daily at 6 a.m. from Wednesday to Sunday. The beach is closed on Mondays and Tuesdays to allow the fish to feed without the interruption of visitors.

What Events to Enjoy on the Island of Oahu

The King Kamehameha Floral Parade

The King Kamehameha Floral Parade is an annual event to honor King Kamehameha I. This event occurs on King Kamehameha I Day (June 11) and features Hawaii's largest parades. After the parade, everyone goes to Kapiolani Park, where they can enjoy music and food between 11 a.m. and 4 p.m.

The Honolulu Festival

The Honolulu Festival is a significant cultural event that aims to celebrate the rich diversity of Pacific Rim cultures. This three-day festival happens annually in March, and you will get to watch several traditional and contemporary performances from Tahiti, Japan, Australia, Taiwan, South Korea, and the Philippines.

O'ahu: Hawai'i Walls

O'ahu: Hawai'i Walls (formerly known as POW! WOW!) is an annual event for art lovers. At this week-long event, you can watch artists in action as they create public art at various locations around Oahu.

Prince Lot Hula Festival

The Prince Lot Hula Festival is an annual event to honor and commemorate Prince Lot Kapuaiwa, who helped revive hula in the 19th century. During this event, you will be able to watch various contemporary and traditional styles of hula dancing.

Where to Eat on the Island of Oahu

Mina's Fish House

Address: 92-1001 Olani St, Kapolei, HI 96707

Hours of operation: 3 p.m. to 9 p.m. daily (dinner is served between 5 p.m. and 9 p.m.)

If you're staying at the Four Seasons and want a nice night out without going far, check out Mina's Fish House. Owned and operated by Chef Michael Mina, you'll find an array of seafood and fish options at this establishment, which you can enjoy as you take in the beautiful views of the ocean. Prices are about mid-range for the food (but worth every bite).

Koko Head Café

Address: 1120 12th Ave #100, Honolulu, HI 96816

Hours of operation: 7 a.m. to 2 p.m. daily

Koko Head Café is a popular place to go if you love brunch! You'll find a great menu at this establishment with many breakfast classics, some with a Hawaiian twist. They also have vegetarian, vegan, and gluten-free options for those who require them.

The Pig and the Lady

Address: 83 N King St, Honolulu, HI 96817

Hours of operation: The Pig and the Lady is open between Monday and Saturday from 11:30 a.m. to 2:30 p.m. and 5:30 p.m. to 9 p.m.

If you're craving some Vietnamese food, the Pig and the Lady is a great place to go. This restaurant serves some classics, including pho and banh mi. However, if you want to try other great options, their Cajun Oyster Po'Boy is a popular menu choice.

Senia

Address: 75 N King St, Honolulu, HI 96817

Hours of operation: 5:30 p.m. to 9:30 p.m., Tuesday to Saturday; tasting menu is on Friday and Saturday at 6:30 p.m.

The atmosphere at Senia is an exciting way to eat as they aim to gather people and friends together to enjoy a meal. This restaurant has an a la carte menu that features plenty of Hawaiian and Asian flavors using high-quality ingredients. Prices are mid-to-high range for their food, with some options for sharing larger plates.

If you're going for the tasting menu, space is limited to eight people. This intimate experience will take you behind the scenes with Chef Anthony Rush and the culinary team.

Marugame Udon

Address: 2310 Kūhiō Ave, Honolulu, HI 96815

Hours of operation: 10 a.m. to 9:30 p.m. daily

If you love udon noodles, you'll want to check out Marugame Udon. This establishment serves these classic, chewy noodles in several options, including the classic kitsune and more adventurous curry options. This restaurant also has tempura, rice bowls, and salads.

Sunrise Shack

Address: 2335 Kalākaua Ave, Honolulu, HI 96815

Hours of operation: 6 a.m. to 7 p.m. daily

If you're looking for a light, healthy breakfast or snack, a visit to the Sunrise Shack is a great option. This establishment was opened up by some surfers looking to provide healthy choices for others. Some of the menu options you can find here include açai bowls, smoothies, and vegan sandwiches.

Over Easy

Address: 418 Kuulei Rd #103, Kailua, HI 96734

Hours of operation :

Wednesday to Friday: 7 a.m. to 1 p.m.

Saturday to Sunday: 7 a.m. to 1:30 p.m.

If you love all-day breakfast, check out Over Easy. This establishment offers delicious breakfast menu options with some Hawaiian flavors. They also have some lunch menu options, too, including burgers. There is also a kids' menu if you are planning a family trip.

Noe

Address: 92-1001 Olani St, Kapolei, HI 96707

Hours of operation: 5 p.m. to 9 p.m. daily

Noe is an Italian option in the Four Seasons Resort featuring a formal dining atmosphere. This restaurant has some tremendous housemade pasta options. However, plenty of other great dishes are on the menu, including the mouth-watering duck breast. This restaurant also has vegan and gluten-free options.

If you want a more intimate experience, Noe has a tasting menu with four courses.

Leonard's Bakery

Address: 933 Kapahulu Ave, Honolulu, HI 96816

Hours of operation: 5:30 a.m. to 7 p.m. daily

Who doesn't want a little sweet treat every once in a while? At Leonard's Bakery, you'll find some delicious Portuguese baked goods, including the classic malasada. This bakery also has wraps, cookies, and freshly baked bread.

Matsumoto Shave Ice

Address: 66-111 Kamehameha Hwy #605, Haleiwa, HI 96712

Hours of operation: 10 a.m. to 6 p.m. daily

Since shaved ice is a classic sweet treat in Hawaii, Matsumoto is one of the best places to grab yourself some if you're on the island of Oahu. The menu is extensive, and everything is made fresh daily.

What to Eat on the Island of Ohau

Garlic Shrimp

Oahu is famous for its garlic shrimp trucks, which serve up succulent shrimp cooked in a garlicky butter sauce and served over a bed of rice. This delicious and indulgent dish is a must-try for seafood lovers and is often enjoyed with a side of macaroni salad or coleslaw.

Spam Musubi

Spam musubi is a popular snack or quick meal consisting of a slice of grilled Spam (canned meat) placed on top of a block of rice and wrapped together with a strip of nori (seaweed). It's a convenient and portable snack that's beloved by locals and visitors alike.

Huli Huli Chicken

Huli huli chicken is a flavorful Hawaiian barbecue dish made by marinating chicken in a tangy sauce (often made with soy sauce, brown sugar, ginger, and garlic) and then grilling it until tender and caramelized. The name "huli huli" comes from the Hawaiian word for

Hawaiian Plate Lunch

A Hawaiian plate lunch typically consists of a protein (such as kalua pork, teriyaki chicken, or mahi-mahi), two scoops of rice, and macaroni salad, all served together on a single plate. It's a popular and convenient meal option that's perfect for sampling a variety of Hawaiian flavors in one dish.

Where to Stay on the Island of Oahu

Four Seasons Ko Olina

Address: 92-1001 Olani St, Ko Olina Resort, Kapolei, HI 96707

This Four Seasons resort is a luxury option but also excellent if you are planning a Hawaiian trip with your family. At this hotel, you can expect world-class hospitality from the staff, a great spa to relax in, and several pools to enjoy (including a kids' one). Kids also dine free if they are under four at the restaurants.

Marriott's Ko Olina Beach Club

Address: 92-161 Waipahe Pl, Ko'Olina Resort, Kapolei, HI 96707

The Marriott Ko Olina Beach Club is another excellent option for families. At this hotel, you'll find spacious villas with full kitchens. If you want to go out for a meal, there are plenty of low-key options in the area, too. This accommodation also has a kids' pool.

Hilton Hawaiian Village Waikiki Resort

Address: 2005 Kalia Rd, Waikiki, Honolulu, HI 96815

The Hilton Hawaiian Village Waikiki Resort is set along the oceanfront and is perfect if you are looking for somewhere to relax. This hotel has plenty of activities for you and your family, including games and crafts. If you want to spend time on the beach but don't want to worry about the waves, the hotel has its own lagoon to swim in.

The Royal Hawaiian

Address: 2259 Kalakaua Ave, Waikiki, Honolulu, HI 96815

The Royal Hawaiian has been a staple accommodation in Honolulu. This hotel dates back to the 1920s and has interesting interior decor. There are plenty of activities for you and your family to enjoy while staying here, including storytelling and hula. There is also a playground, water slide, and interactive fountain for kids to play.

Ala Moana Hotel

Address: 410 Atkinson Dr, Honolulu, HI 96814

Ala Moana Hotel is a bit more budget-friendly for those seeking comfort and convenience in the heart of Honolulu. This hotel is next to the famous Ala Moana Shopping Center and Ala Moana Beach Park, making it easy to access recreational activities and shopping. Some rooms have views of the ocean, while others overlook the city.

White Sands Hotel

Address: 431 Nohonani St, Honolulu, HI, 96815

The White Sands Hotel boasts some 1960s flare with its retro-styled rooms. At this budget-friendly accommodation, you'll find yourself close to the beach and local attractions, including Waikiki Beach. Many are big fans of the bar on the pool deck, which has some swings to sit on while you sip your beverage. If you are traveling to Hawaii with family, this hotel has family rooms and children's cots if you need one.

Disney's Aulani Resort and Spa

Address: 92-1185 Aliinui Dr, Kapolei, HI 96707

Who doesn't love a themed resort, especially if you're a big Disney lover? At the Disney Aulani Resort and Spa, this family-friendly resort is along a lagoon with a stunning white sand beach. There is plenty of Disney magic throughout the resort: water slides, a lazy river, and activities for kids. Of course, it wouldn't be a Disney resort without seeing some Disney characters! You have a few room options at Disney Aulani, including resort rooms, villas, and suites.

Ewa Hotel Waikiki

Address: 2555 Cartwright Rd, Waikiki, Honolulu, HI 96815

Staying at the Ewa Hotel Waikiki will provide a convenient base from which to explore Honolulu and its beaches without breaking the bank. This hotel is close to Waikiki Beach and has dining, shopping, and other entertainment options. Additionally, Ewa Hotel Waikiki has an on-site pool to enjoy that provides excellent views of the Pacific Ocean. As for rooms, this hotel has family options, and all rooms are equipped with a fridge.

Aqua Palms Waikiki

Address: 1850 Ala Moana Blvd, Waikiki, Honolulu, HI 96815

At the Aqua Palm Waikiki, you can expect comfort and convenience. This hotel is within walking distance of Waikiki Beach and several other attractions. All rooms have microwaves and mini-fridges.

AC Hotel by Marriott Honolulu

Address: 1111 Bishop St, Honolulu, HI 96813

AC Hotel by Marriott Honolulu is in the city's center, putting you close to Waikiki Beach, shopping, and dining. This hotel offers spacious rooms with some overlooking the ocean. There is a rooftop pool you can enjoy, with panoramic views of Honolulu and the ocean and plenty of on-site dining options.

What Not to Do on the Island of Oahu

Be Respectful at Pearl Harbor National Memorial

Show reverence and respect for the memorial and its significance by observing quiet and respectful behavior. Dress respectfully for your visit to the memorial, avoiding clothing with offensive language or imagery and adhering to any dress code requirements. Avoid bringing large bags or backpacks into the memorial, as they may not be allowed inside certain areas or may require additional security screening. Use discretion when taking photos, especially at solemn locations such as the USS Arizona Memorial, and avoid posing inappropriately or taking selfies. Show respect for commemorative spaces and memorials by refraining from loud conversations, disruptive behavior, or inappropriate gestures. Take time to learn about the historical significance of Pearl Harbor and the events of December 7, 1941, to fully appreciate the memorial's importance.

Don't Rush your visit to Byodo-In Temple.

Plan to spend at least 3-4 hours at Byodo-In Temple to soak in the spiritual rejuvenation. This place can bring solace and peace of mind. Be mindful of ongoing religious practices or ceremonies and avoid disrupting them with loud noises or disruptive behavior. Refrain from touching or climbing on temple structures, statues, or artifacts to preserve their integrity and cultural significance. Follow proper etiquette by removing your shoes before entering the temple or any designated areas where shoes are not allowed.

Don't Walk Alone at Night in Oahu

The island of Oahu is generally safe. However, areas like downtown Honolulu, Waipahu, and Waianae tend to see more criminal activity at night. Always be mindful of your surroundings, and if you can avoid walking alone at night, do so!

Don't Assume There Won't Be Resort Fees

Resort fees are in place to help cover things like the internet and pool maintenance. Remember to research how much resort fees are when looking at accommodation options to ensure they fit within your budget, as they are added per night.

Next Stop: The Island of Kauai

Oahu is one of the more well-known islands in Hawaii. It is the place of Pearl Harbor, where America saw one of the worst days in history, and has many famous beaches, including Waikiki. As you continue to plan and research your trip, you now have a list of great places to explore on this Hawaiian Island so that you can make the most of your trip if you choose to visit Oahu. In the next chapter, we'll go to Kauai Island to explore its attractions and what to avoid.

Chapter 7:
Kauai Island—Dos and Don'ts

Did you know that Kauai has a palm tree building code? Compared to the other Hawaiian Islands, Kauai is the one island that does not have any skyscrapers, and that is because it's illegal to have buildings that are taller than the palm trees! This means you won't see tall hotels, resorts, or other buildings past four stories, preserving the beauty of Kauai's landscape.

Discovering the Island of Kauai

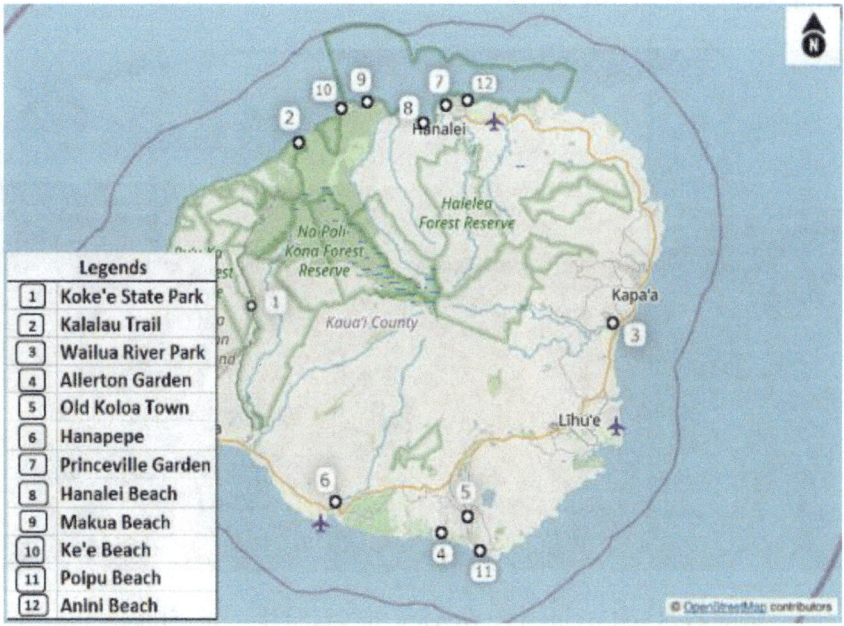

Kauai, also known as the Garden Isle, is the oldest and fourth-largest in the chain of Hawaiian Islands. As with the other islands, Kauai's history dates back to the arrival of the Polynesian settlers who flourished there. When Captain James Cook visited Hawaii in the late 1770s, this brought in European influence and trading. Kauai also became an influential island for its agriculture, especially since parts of the island have enough rain to help plants grow and flourish.

This island boasts dramatic landscapes, including the soaring cliffs of the Na Pali Coast, the stunning Waimea Canyon, and the many lush tropical forests throughout. Many landmarks are worth seeing, including the Allerton Garden, Old Koloa Town, and the Princeville Botanical Gardens.

As this island has seen many different settlers call Kauai home, you'll find a blend of Hawaiian traditions, Asian influences, and modern-day lifestyles meshed together, making this island a beautiful and unique one to visit.

What to Do on the Island of Kauai

Koke'e State Park and Waimea Canyon

Address: Hanapepe, HI 96716

Koke'e State Park and Waimea Canyon are the Grand Canyon of the Pacific. This state park is spread across 4,325 acres and has plenty of things to do for those who love the outdoors. This park has 18 trails you can hike to explore the diverse landscapes, including rainforests and towering cliffs that will give you panoramic views of the canyon and surrounding coastline. The park also has two great lookouts that offer stunning views of the Kalalau Valley. The temperatures drop if you climb these lookout areas, so ensure you have a warm layer.

In addition to hiking and exploring Koke'e State Park, you can camp or rent one of their cabins.

Entrance type	Price
General Admission	$5
Children under three	Free

Parking fees are $10 for noncommercial vehicles.

If you intend to camp here, you can book campsites as early as 90 days in advance, and they are $30 per night.

The Kalalau Trail

The Kalalau Trail is one of the most famous hikes in the world, renowned for its breathtaking beauty and challenging terrain. This trail dates back to the 1800s and is the only way to reach the Na Pali Coast by foot and land. This trail is a 22-mile round trip, and hiking the 11 miles will take about a day, depending on your fitness level. If you intend to do the full 22-mile round hike and camp along the way, you must have a camping permit, and you can only camp at Hanakoa or Kalalau. To access the trailhead, you must be in Hā'ena State Park.

Wailua River State Park

Address: Kapa'a, HI 96746

Hours of operation: 7 a.m. to 7:45 p.m.

Wailua River State Park is one of Kauai's natural gems, with the most scenic river that will bring you through a stunning tropical landscape and ancient Hawaiian cultural sites, including the remains of heiau and pu'uhonua (places of worship and refuge) and ancient birthing stones. This is the state park where you can also see the Fern Grotto, which is only accessible by boat. The park has no admission fees, and you can rent kayaks or paddle boards from the Kayak Kauai. It's best to get to the park early to ensure you can get parking.

Allerton and McBryde Gardens

Address: 4425 Lawai Rd, Koloa, HI 96756

Allerton and McBryde Gardens is a botanical paradise filled with exotic flowers, dramatic fig trees, and other plant species. The Allerton Garden was once the private estate of Queen Emma. Robert Allerton and John Gregg Allerton further developed it in the late 1930s by adding various garden rooms and water features. McBryde Garden, adjacent to Allerton, showcases an impressive array of tropical plants, including rare and endangered species worldwide.

The Allerton Garden Guided Tour

The Allerton Guided tour is part garden tour and part art exhibit, where you'll be brought through beautiful garden rooms with sculptures, water features, and exotic plants. This tour is 2.5 hours and takes place on Tuesdays, Thursdays, and Saturdays.

What NOT To Do - Hawaii

Ticket type	Price
Adults (13 years old and up)	$65
Children (2 to 12 years old)	$32.50
Infants	Free

The Allerton Garden at Sunset Tour

The Allerton Garden at Sunset Tour will bring you through a selection of garden rooms and the Allerton house, where you can see a collection of pictures and memorabilia. At the end of your tour, you'll enjoy a beverage while watching the sunset. This tour is three hours long and takes place on Wednesdays, Fridays, and Saturdays.

Ticket type	Price
Adults (13 years old and up)	$105
Children (6 to 12 years old)	$60
Children (2 to 5 years old)	$30
Infants	Free

Best of Both Worlds

During this 2.5-hour tour, you will get a behind-the-scenes tour that will bring you through some of Allerton's garden rooms and some of the highlights from the McBryde Garden. This tour takes place between Tuesday and Sunday.

Ticket type	Price
Adults (13 years old and up)	$65
Children (2 to 12 years old)	$32.50
Infants	Free

Allerton by Fire

Allerton by Fire is a dinner tour served at the Allerton Estate. This luau is a fun experience as it has live Polynesian dancing, music, and a fire knife performance. This experience only happens on Tuesdays and Thursdays.

Ticket type	Price
Adults (13 years old and up)	$175
Children (2 to 12 years old)	$150
Infants	Free

McBryde Garden Self-Guided Tour

Ticket type	Price
Adults (13 years old and up)	$30
Children (2 to 12 years old)	$15
Infants	Free

Old Kōloa Town

Old Kōloa Town is on Kauai's southern coast. It holds significant historical importance in Hawaii as it was the site of the first commercial sugar plantation opened by Ladd and Company in 1835. This first shaped the economy for sugar production across Hawaii's other islands and opened the door to new immigrants, making Hawaii their home and creating the diverse country it is today.

Old Kōloa has retained much of its historic charm today, with its old-fashioned storefronts and plantation-era buildings. The Kōloa History Center is open between 9 a.m. and 9 p.m., which is worth paying a visit to as it has plenty of displays and information about the town's history.

Hanapepe

The town of Hanapepe is a must-visit when you go to the island of Kauai. Known as "Kauai's Biggest Little Town," this town was bustling during the 1930s and World War II. Unfortunately, it did see a significant decline in the 1970s and 1980s, as well as devastation from Hurricane Iniki in 1992. The historic buildings were rebuilt after the hurricane, and you can explore this charming town with its plantation-style buildings lining the main street and stroll across the Hanapepe Swinging Bridge that offers breathtaking views of the Hanapepe River below. Additionally, the town hosts a weekly Hanapepe Art Night every Friday from 6 p.m. to 9 p.m., showcasing the vibrant local arts scene.

Princeville Botanical Gardens

Address: 3840 Ahonui Pl, Princeville, HI, 96722

Hidden in the lush landscape of Kauai's north shore is the Princeville Botanical Gardens, a stunning oasis that started as a hobby to Lucinda and Bill Robertson in 2001. These gardens were once cattle lands. The Robertsons worked hard to remove invasive species that took away the native flora by supplementing the soil with homemade compost and organic fertilizers. At this garden, you'll be guided by a knowledgeable guide to see the diverse plant species, exotic flowers, and fruit trees. You'll also get to taste the chocolate and honey from their beehives.

Three-Hour Walking and Chocolate Tasting Tour

Ticket type	Price
Adults (14 years old and up)	$95
Children (3 to 13 years old)	$40
Children 2 and under	Free

The Island of Kauai's Beaches

Hanalei Beach and Bay

If this beach looks familiar to you, you're right! Hanalei Beach Park and Bay was featured in Alexander Payne's 2011 film, The Descendants, starring George Clooney and Shailene Woodley. This beautiful gold and white sand beach faces the west, making it a lovely spot to go and watch the sunset.

Hanalei Bay is also a great place to go if you love water sports. The conditions are perfect for kayaking, stand-up paddle boarding, and swimming during the summer. You might even dare to jump off the pier if you're brave enough! This is a great place to spend the day basking in the sun while getting some adventure in, too!

Makua Beach

Makua Beach is another great beach for stunning sunset views and stunning views of the Na Pali Coast. This beach, also known as the Tunnels Beach, earned its nickname for its distinctive underwater lava tubes, which create a unique snorkeling experience among the colorful coral reefs and marine life. The beach's waters are also calm, making it great for swimming, exploring, and participating in other water sports during the summer.

If you happen to be planning your Hawaiian trip between November and March, this beach will be closed due to the dangerous conditions.

Ke'e Beach

Ke'e Beach is one of Kauai's best beaches to visit. This beach is in the Ha'ena State Park, surrounded by craggy cliffs and a dense jungle. To see this beach, you'll need to reserve your day pass with Ha'ena State Park. This ensures that the beach and park are not overcrowded with visitors.

There are three options for entering Ha'ena State Park: shuttle and entry, parking and entry, and entry only.

Shuttle and Entry
Shuttle tickets are a round trip. They run daily, starting at 6:20 a.m. until 5:40 p.m.

Ticket type	Price
Adults (16 years old and up)	$40
Children (4 to 15 years old)	$25
Children 3 and under	Free

Parking and Entry

Parking and entering Ha'ena State Park is $10 plus a $5 per entry fee. You must purchase multiple time slots to spend the day at the park. Otherwise, it would be best if you were out of the park by the end of your time slot. The parking times are as follows:

- Morning: 6:30 a.m. to 12:30 p.m.
- Afternoon: 12:30 p.m. to 5:30 p.m.
- Evening: 4:30 p.m. to sunset.

Entry Only

If you only pay the entry fee, it is $5 per person. However, this is only if you're biking or have another mode of transportation that does not require parking a car. You cannot park outside of the park. It will result in a $200 minimum ticket plus being towed.

Poipu Beach

Poipu Beach is another famous beach located on the south side of Kauai. This beautiful beach is renowned for its golden sands, turquoise waters, and calm conditions, making it perfect for swimming, snorkeling, and other water activities—even in the winter! This beach is also near several restaurants and has plenty of parking!

Anini Beach

Anini Beach is tucked along the beautiful north shore of Kauai, well-loved for its tranquil waters and stunning scenery. What sets this beach apart from the others we have discussed is that it has a protective offshore reef that has made a shallow lagoon ideal for swimming, especially if you are traveling to Kauai with your family and have littles in tow. The calm conditions make it a perfect destination for paddle boarding and snorkeling to explore marine life.

What Events to Enjoy on the Island of Kauai

Kōloa Plantation Days Festival

The Kōloa Plantation Days Festival is a celebration annually in July, paying homage to Kauai's sugar plantation heritage. This 10-day festival has various events and activities to immerse yourself in, including live musical performances and dances, a rodeo, a parade, and plenty of food.

Kauai Mokihana Festival

The Kauai Mokihana Festival is a week-long event on the island that is held every September. During this festival, you can immerse yourself in various events, including Hawaiian musical concerts, hula performances, workshops, and a craft fair. Admission for the multiple events you can go to start around $20.

Eō E ʻEmalani I Alakaʻi Festival

The Eō E ʻEmalani I Alakaʻi Festival is an event that celebrates the life and legacy of Queen Emma, also known as Queen Emma Kalanikaumakaamano Kaleleonalani Naea Rooke of Hawaii. This festival happens annually in October and features various cultural performances, educational exhibits, craft vendors, and food stalls. This festival takes place at the Kokee State Park, and it's best to arrive early in the day to ensure you get a good parking spot.

Kauai Marathon and Half Marathon

If you're a runner, this might be a great event in Hawaii in September. The Kauai Marathon and Half Marathon allow you to challenge yourself as you run through some of Kauai's most scenic routes along the coastline, taking in some of Kauai's picturesque beaches, rainforests, and volcanic peaks.

Waimea Town Celebration

The Waimea Town Celebration is a nine-day celebration that takes place every February. You'll enjoy many activities and events at this celebration, including live musical performances, hula dances, and local food vendors providing delicious Hawaiian cuisine. There are also arts and crafts exhibitions and sporting events, such as canoe races. This is one of Waimea's oldest events and is worth visiting to immerse yourself in Hawaii's rich cultural heritage.

Where to Eat on the Island of Kauai

Hukilau Lanai

Address: Kauai Coast Resort, 520 Aleka Lp, Kapa'a, HI 96746

Hours of operation: Tuesday to Saturday from 5 p.m. to 9 p.m.

Hukilau Lanai is an upscale restaurant with some of the best seafood dishes on the island. This establishment uses locally sourced ingredients to create dishes with inspired Hawaiian flavors. Everything is made fresh, and they have something that will cater to anyone's dietary needs, including a kids' menu.

Duke's Kauai

Address: 3610 Rice St, Lihue, HI 96766

Hours of operation

- Monday to Saturday: 11 a.m. to 10 p.m.
- Sunday: 9 a.m. to 10 p.m.

Duke's Kauai serves traditional Hawaiian and classic American dishes in the Marriott's Kauai Beach Club. Everything is made with locally sourced ingredients, and some of their popular options include poke tacos, fish tacos, and Duke's famous Hula Pie. Even if you don't have the time to sit down and eat, or maybe you're looking for a quick drink at the bar, this restaurant has a great cocktail menu, especially if you love piña coladas or mai tais.

Bar Acuda

Address: 5-5161 Kuhio Hwy, Hanalei, HI 96714

Hours of operation: Tuesday to Saturday from 5:30 p.m. to 9:30 p.m.

At Bar Acuda, this menu focuses on creating and serving farm-to-table dishes bursting with flavor. All meals are made from locally sourced and fresh ingredients. If you do eat here, you can expect the prices to be on the higher side. It's also a popular establishment, so if you plan to eat here, you'll want to make reservations as early as possible.

Palate Wine Bar and Restaurant

Address: 2474 Keneke St, Kilauea, HI 96754

Hours of operation: 5 p.m. to 8:30 p.m. daily

Palate Wine Bar and Restaurant offers an intimate dining experience within its small establishment. This restaurant serves small tapa dishes and regular-sized meals, making it perfect to share or indulge. As this is a wine bar, you can expect some of the best wine selections to pair with your meal.

Kalaheo Cafe and Coffee Company

Address: 2-2560 Kaumualii Hwy, Kalaheo, HI 96741

Hours of operation: Wednesday to Sunday from 7 a.m. to 2 p.m.

Kalaheo Cafe and Coffee Company is another great establishment to pop into if you're looking for a cup of coffee or a quick bite to eat. This cafe is a cozy spot in Kalaheo, offering pancakes, omelets, and burrito wraps or bowls in addition to coffee, smoothies, teas, and juice.

Anakēs Juice Bar

Address: 2827 Poipu Rd, Koloa, HI 96756

Hours of operation: Saturday to Thursday from 8 a.m. to 2 p.m.

For another quick bite to eat if you're on the go, check out Anakē's Juice Bar. This little establishment is hidden in the Kukuiula Market and offers freshly squeezed juice, smoothies, and acai bowls.

Ilima Terrace Restaurant

Address: 1571 Poipu Rd, Koloa, HI 96756

Hours of operation: 6 a.m. to 2 p.m. daily

Ilima Terrace Restaurant is located in the Grand Hyatt and is an excellent spot to go if you're looking for breakfast options. This restaurant has a buffet and a la carte options to choose from. You won't find just the basics if you go with the buffet. There are also omelets, breakfast hash, and more. As you eat in the open-air seating area, you'll enjoy the beautiful scenery of their gardens and the Keoneloa Bay.

Sam's Ocean View Restaurant and Bar

Address: 4-1546 Kuhio Hwy, Kapa'a, HI 96746

Hours of operation: Thursday to Monday from 4 p.m. to 9 p.m.

Sam's Ocean View Restaurant and Bar is an excellent establishment if you're looking for a casual night out. This restaurant boasts beautiful ocean views to enjoy as you eat, especially if you're there when the sun is setting! All of their meals are made with locally sourced ingredients, and they have daily fish options that are all delicious. This place tends to book fast, so make reservations as early as possible (especially if you want a table with the best ocean views).

Kountry Kitchen

Address: 4-1489 Kuhio Hwy, Kapa'a, HI 96746

Hours of operation: Thursday to Monday from 7 a.m. to 1 p.m.

Kountry Kitchen is a family-owned restaurant that is popular among the locals. This establishment serves all your favorite breakfast foods, including some that follow traditional Hawaiian flavors, such as loco moco or macadamia nut pancakes served with their homemade coconut syrup.

Small Town Coffee

Address: 4-1543 Kuhio Hwy, Kapa'a, HI 96746

Hours of operation: Monday to Saturday: 6 a.m. to 12 p.m.

If you're a fan of coffee, you will want to stop by Small Town Coffee. This establishment has some of the best coffee on the island and also offers small breakfast sandwiches and pastries made in-house.

What to Eat on the Island of Kauai

Ahi Poke

Ahi poke is a popular Hawaiian dish made with cubed raw yellowfin tuna (ahi) marinated in a mixture of soy sauce, sesame oil, green onions, and other seasonings. It's a delicious and refreshing dish that highlights the fresh flavors of the fish and is often served as an appetizer or snack.

Haupia

Haupia is a traditional Hawaiian coconut pudding made with coconut milk, sugar, and cornstarch. It has a smooth and creamy texture with a subtle coconut flavor and is often served chilled as a dessert. Haupia is a refreshing and light way to end a meal and is enjoyed by both locals and visitors alike.

Poi

Poi is a traditional Hawaiian staple made from taro root, which is cooked and mashed, and then water is added to achieve the desired consistency. It's often served as a side dish alongside main courses like kalua pig or lomilomi salmon. Poi can vary in texture from thick to thin and in flavor from slightly sweet to tangy.

Shave Ice

Shave ice is a popular Hawaiian dessert made by shaving ice into a fine, fluffy texture and then topping it with flavored syrups. On Kauai, you'll find shave ice stands offering a wide variety of flavors, including traditional options like strawberry, pineapple, and coconut, as well as unique combinations like lilikoi (passion fruit) and haupia (coconut cream).

Where to Stay on the Island of Kauai

The Westin Princeville Ocean Resort Villas

Address: Vistana, 3838 Wyllie Rd, Princeville, HI 96722

The Westin Princeville Ocean Resort Villas is a stunning luxury resort boasting ocean views from some villas. This resort has studio-sized and one- and two-bedroom villa options, which is perfect if you will be traveling to Hawaii with your family. This resort has four pools and a great farm-to-table restaurant on site. However, the studio and villas also have fully equipped kitchens. This resort also has a spa and a large fitness center.

Hanalei Colony Resort

Address: 5 7130 Kuhio Hwy, Hanalei, HI 96714

Hanalei Colony Resort is a three-star hotel with spacious suites that offer ocean views. The hotel is right along the beach, giving guests easy access to the water outside the resort. However, if you want to visit other beaches in the area, Hanalei Colony Resort offers complimentary guest shuttle services. If you have rented a car, parking is free. There are also coin-operated laundry facilities.

Grand Hyatt Kauai Resort and Spa

Address: 1571 Poipu Rd, Koloa, HI 96756

Set within 50 acres of lush gardens, the Grand Hyatt Kauai Resort and Spa is an excellent accommodation for a private and serene retreat for your Hawaiian adventure. This hotel has several amenities, including a lazy river, a yoga room, and family-friendly activities. Guests love this hotel for the many views from the rooms, including mountains, the ocean, and the pool.

Hilton Garden Inn Wailua Bay

Address: 3-5920 Kuhio Hwy, Kapa'a, HI 96746

The Hilton Garden Inn Wailua Bay is an excellent option for those seeking luxury and convenience. This hotel is set along Wailua Bay and boasts stunning views of the Pacific Ocean and easy access to the beaches. The Hilton Garden Inn and Wailua Bay rooms are modern and equipped with the amenities you'll need for a comfortable stay. This accommodation does have a resort fee, which includes two daily refills of bottled water, two soft drinks, two-hour bike rentals, a cultural sunrise ceremony, a beach towel and mat, and yoga classes.

Waimea Plantation Cottages

Address: 9400 Kaumualii Hwy, Waimea, HI 96796

The Waimea Plantation Cottages are an excellent option for those who don't want to stay at a resort. These quaint cottages date back to the 1900s, are spacious, have fully equipped kitchens, and are a short walk to the private beach on the property. This accommodation is also a short walk from the downtown area of Waimea, making it excellent for picking up essentials.

Makai Club Resort

Address: 4180 Lei O Papa Rd, Princeville, HI 96722

Makai Club Resort is on a beautiful hillside alongside the Makai Golf Course. At this accommodation, the rooms are bright and spacious and come with fully-equipped kitchens to make you feel right at home. They also provide beach chairs and umbrellas to use at the beach and are within walking distance of the grocery store. This hotel does have a daily and nightly resort fee to keep in mind if you book a room here.

Kauai Palms Hotel

Address: 2931 Kalena St, Lihue, HI 96766

Kauai Palms Hotel is not a luxury, but it has spacious and bright rooms to suit your traveling needs. This hotel is near downtown, the Kauai Lagoons Golf Club, and Kalapaki Bay. Several room options are available, including cottage and studio options.

OUTRIGGER Kauai Beach Resort and Spa

Address: 4331 Kauai Beach Dr, Lihue, HI 96766

Staying at OUTRIGGER Kauai Beach Resort and Spa is a treat-yourself vacation. This resort offers a tranquil escape if you're looking for a mixture of rejuvenation and adventure as it boasts many spa treatments, including beach massages, as well as being within proximity to the Na Pali Coast and Waimea Canyon, making it an ideal base for exploring Kauai's beauty. Some additional perks of staying at this accommodation include four outdoor pools, a children's pool, and evening entertainment.

Aston Islander on the Beach

Address: 440 Aleka Pl, Kapaa, HI 96746

Aston Islander on the Beach is along the Coconut Coast in Kauai. This stunning resort is located along a gorgeous white sand beach with an oceanfront pool and hot tub where you can enjoy the beautiful scenery. Some rooms also have a balcony with partial or complete ocean views. Aston Islander on the Beach is within walking distance of several attractions, including the Wailua River State Park and the Kapaa Lookout.

The Cliffs at Princeville

Address: 3811 Edward Rd, Princeville, HI 96722

The Cliffs at Princeville is a three-star resort on the north shore of Kauai. This accommodation has two hot tubs, a swimming pool, and a children's pool. All the rooms are spacious, with two private balconies, a full kitchen, and laundry facilities. While staying here, you can use the tennis courts, a pickleball court, a half-basketball court, and their two shuffleboards. For exploring the island, The Cliffs are a short drive away from various attractions, including the Na Pali Coast and Anini Beach.

What Not to Do on the Island of Kauai

Don't Swim in Queen's Bath if It's Unsafe

Queen's Bath is a natural tide pool in Princeville. It's a scenic spot known for its crystal-clear waters and unique geological formations, mainly since the pool itself was formed by lava rock. When the tide is low, it becomes a bathing area where many love to swim and relax. However, while it can be calm, especially during the summer, it can become quite dangerous, especially in the winter or when the ocean conditions are rough. If you plan to visit, remember to exercise caution and check the surf conditions, as it's only worth the hike if the waves are under four feet.

Don't Hike on Illegal Trails

You may find some areas in Kauai are marked with no trespassing signs. Don't ignore the postage signage when going hiking on these trails. They are posted for a reason.

Avoid These Areas on Kauai

Some areas on Kauai aren't as pleasant and should be avoided due to rougher crowds. Therefore, you should avoid going to Lyndgate, Hanalei Pavilion, and Salt Pond while on the island of Kauai.

Embrace the Aloha

On the island of Kauai, you'll find plenty of things to see and do in this lush Garden Isle. From enjoying the beautiful beaches where you can swim in the calm water and bask in the sun to adventuring and exploring the state parks and gardens, this island is truly magical in its way that will leave you feeling inspired to embrace the aloha spirit. We have now gone through the Hawaiian Islands and the things to see and do on them. Now, it's up to you to decide where to go and what to see to make your Hawaiian vacation your own.

Conclusion

Planning your dream Hawaiian getaway is just getting started. Throughout this book, we have explored everything you need to plan your trip, from learning about the peak travel times to how to get there and between the islands if you're not settling down on one for your vacation. We also explored the planning tips and tricks for your Hawaiian itinerary and how to get around the islands.

Hawaii has many beautiful islands to explore, some of which are vibrant and others that provide a sense of tranquility. On each Hawaiian Island, there is something to see and do. From the Big Island's Volcanoes National Park to the quaint plantation villages on the island of Kauai, you get to see how much Hawaii has changed over the years. However, beyond the attractions and things to see, Hawaii's diverse landscape, with its lush rainforests and crystal clear waters in the Pacific Ocean, leaves the door open for discovery and learning. It's also a place of reflection if you visit historic sites like Pearl Harbor, where you can see the sunken USS Arizona.

Beyond its stunning scenery, Hawaii's vibrant culture is one to experience whenever possible, especially with traditional hula performances and the local cuisine influenced by diverse cultures, including Asian and Polynesian. These experiences and the many festivals and events throughout the year allow you to immerse yourself in the aloha spirit, especially when you join tours that dive deeper into this profound meaning of life in Hawaii. Hawaii's history has always been fascinating, especially since it didn't officially join the United States until the 1950s, making it the most unique state to visit.

With Hawaii's warm hospitality, breathtaking scenery, and endless experiences, this journey will leave a lasting impression, no matter which island or combination of islands you choose to visit on your trip. Now that you have everything you need to plan your trip, all that is left is for you to get there and enjoy Hawaii's beautiful landscapes and its rich culture and history.

If this book has helped you plan your trip to Hawaii, leave the gift of the aloha spirit by leaving a review on Amazon.

References

A brief history of Moloka'i. (2020, July 8). Molokini Crater. https://molokinicrater.com/brief-history-molokai
A brief history of the Hula. (2018, February 1). Hawaii Ocean Project. https://hawaiioceanproject.com/a-brief-history-of-the-hula
About HBC. (n.d.). Hilo Bay Cafe. https://hilobaycafe.com/about
About the course. (n.d.). The Kauai Marathon & Half Marathon. https://thekauaimarathon.com/the-race/the-course
About us. (n.d.-a). Da Poke Shack. https://dapokeshack.com/about-us
About us. (n.d.-b). Big Island Brewhaus. https://bigislandbrewhaus.com/about-big-island-brewhaus
About us. (n.d.-c). Hilo Bay Oceanfront Bed & Breakfast. https://www.hilobayoceanfront.com/about
About us. (n.d.-d). Princeville Botanical Gardens. https://kauaibotanicalgardens.com/about-us
AC Hotel by Marriott Honolulu. (n.d.). Booking.com. https://www.booking.com/hotel/us/ac-by-marriott-honolulu.en-gb.html
Accommodations. (n.d.-a). Volcano House. https://hawaiivolcanohouse.com/accomodations
Accommodations. (n.d.-b). The Hawaiian Islands. https://www.gohawaii.com/islands/lanai/accommodations
Activities. (n.d.). Dole Plantation. https://www.doleplantation.com/activities
admin. (2023, February 1). *When is the best time to visit Hawaii?* Collections of Waikīkī. https://collectionsofwaikiki.com/best-time-to-visit-hawaii
Ahuena Heiau. (n.d.). HawaiianIslands.com. https://hawaiianislands.com/big-island/things-to-do/ahuena-heiau
Ahupua`a o Molokai. (2017, April 20). *Kuhio Day Celebration.* The Molokai Dispatch. https://themolokaidispatch.com/kuhio-day-celebration
'Akaka Falls State Park. (n.d.). Hawaii.gov. https://dlnr.hawaii.gov/dsp/parks/hawaii/akaka-falls-state-park
Ala Moana Hotel - resort fee included. (n.d.). Booking.com. https://www.booking.com/hotel/us/ala-moana-en-gb.html
Allerton & McBryde Gardens. (n.d.). The Hawaiian Islands. https://www.gohawaii.com/islands/kauai/regions/south-shore/allerton-mcbryde-gardens
Aloha! Welcome to Hale Hui Kai. (n.d.). Hale Hui Kai. https://www.halehuikai.com
Aqua Palms Waikiki. (n.d.). Booking.com. https://www.booking.com/hotel/us/aqua-palms-spa.en-gb.html
Aston Islander on the Beach. (n.d.). Booking.com. https://www.booking.com/hotel/us/aston-islander-on-the-beach.en-gb.html
Aston Kaanapali Shores. (n.d.). Booking.com. https://www.booking.com/hotel/us/aston-kaanapali-shores.html
Bailar, T. (2023, July 7). *11 dangerous things and places to avoid in Oahu.* Travel Compositions. https://travelcompositions.com/places-to-avoid-in-oahu
Banana Bungalow Hostel: "You had me at Aloha!" (n.d.). Banana Bungalow Hostel. https://www.mauihostel.com
Bayona, J. A. (Director). (n.d.). *Jurassic world: Fallen kingdom* [Film]. Universal Pictures.
Beaches and water safety. (n.d.). Marine Corps. https://hawaii.usmc-mccs.org/recreation-fitness/beaches
Beal, S. (n.d.-a). *How to see the sea cliffs of Molokai.* Go Visit Hawaii. https://www.govisithawaii.com/2014/10/20/how-to-see-the-sea-cliffs-of-molokai
Beal, S. (n.d.-b). *Maui and Molokai helicopter tours, pricing, and reviews.* Go Visit Hawaii. https://www.govisithawaii.com/2018/07/24/maui-and-molokai-helicopter-tours-pricing-and-reviews
Book a room with ease. (n.d.). The Mauian on Napili Bay. https://www.mauian.com
Briney, A. (2019, April 22). *Geography of Hawaii.* ThoughtCo. https://www.thoughtco.com/geography-of-hawaii-1435728
Brown's Beach House. (n.d.). Fairmont Orchid. https://www.fairmont.com/orchid-hawaii/dining/browns-beach-house
Byodo-In Temple. (n.d.). The Hawaiian Islands. https://www.gohawaii.com/islands/oahu/regions/windward-coast/byodo-in-temple
caitylincoln. (2022, May 17). *Is Molokai worth visiting? Short answer: Yes. But it's unlike any other Hawaiian Island.* Lincoln Travel Co. https://hulalandblog.com/is-molokai-worth-visiting
Cancler, C. (n.d.). *Kauaʻi: Waimea Town celebration 9-day festival with rodeo, hoʻolauleʻa, and contests.* Hawaii on the Cheap. https://hawaiionthecheap.com/kauai-waimea-town-celebration
Cancler, C. (2023, May 6). *Oʻahu: Hawaiʻi Walls 2023 street art (formerly POW! WOW!).* Hawaiʻi on the Cheap. https://hawaiionthecheap.com/event/oahu-hawaii-walls-2023-street-art-formerly-pow-wow
Cheung, M. (2022, September 2). *Eighteen mind-blowing facts about Kauai.* Hawaii Travel with Kids. https://hawaiitravelwithkids.com/facts-about-kauai-you-probably-dont-know
Cheung, M. (2023, March 17). *6 exciting Hawaii Lei Day celebrations + 4 Hawaii activities for kids (2023).* Hawaii Travel with Kids. https://hawaiitravelwithkids.com/hawaiian-lei-day-traditions-activities
Cutforth, D., & Lipsitz, J. (Executive Producers). (2006–present). *Top Chef* [TV Series]. Magical Elves Productions; Bravo.
Derrick, J. C. (n.d.-a). *Maui Kayak Tours.* Hawaii Guide. https://www.hawaii-guide.com/maui/activities/maui-kayak-adventures
Derrick, J. C. (n.d.-b). *Ten places to avoid in Hawaii.* Hawaii Guide. https://www.hawaii-guide.com/10-places-to-avoid-in-hawaii
Derrick, J. C. (n.d.-c). *All about Oahu.* Hawaii Guide. https://www.hawaii-guide.com/oahu/articles/all_about_oahu
Derrick, J. C. (n.d.-d). *All about the Big Island of Hawaii.* Hawaii Guide. https://www.hawaii-guide.com/big-island/all-about-big-island-hawaii
Derrick, J. C. (n.d.-e). *Dole Pineapple Plantation.* Hawaii Guide. https://www.hawaii-guide.com/oahu/sights/dole-plantation
Derrick, J. C. (n.d.-f). *Hanauma Bay.* Hawaii Guide. https://www.hawaii-guide.com/oahu/sights/hanauma-bay
Derrick, J. C. (n.d.-g). *Kona Coast Kekaha Kai State Park Information.* Hawaii Guide. https://www.hawaii-guide.com/big-island/beaches/kona_coast_kekaha_kai_state_park
Derrick, J. C. (n.d.-h). *Maui beaches.* Hawaii Guide. https://www.hawaii-guide.com/maui/beaches
Derrick, J. C. (n.d.-h). *Oahu beaches.* Hawaii Guide. https://www.hawaii-guide.com/oahu/beaches
Derrick, J. C. (n.d.-j). *Oahu, essential things to know.* Hawaii Guide. https://www.hawaii-guide.com/oahu/oahu-things-to-know

Derrick, J. C. (n.d.-k). *Oahu hiking trails.* Hawaii Guide. https://www.hawaii-guide.com/oahu/hiking-trails/manoa-falls-trail

Derrick, J. C. (n.d.-l). *The road to Hana stops.* Hawaii Guide. https://www.hawaii-guide.com/maui/road-to-hana-stops

Derrick, J. C. (n.d.-m). *The ultimate guide to Lanai.* Hawaii Guide. https://www.hawaii-guide.com/lanai/the-ultimate-guide-to-lanai

Derrick, J. C. (n.d.-m). *Turtle Town Maui.* Hawaii Guide. https://www.hawaii-guide.com/maui/beaches/the-magic-of-maluaka-turtle-town

Derrick, V. C. (n.d.). *Waikiki Honolulu region hike.* Hawaii Guide. https://www.hawaii-guide.com/oahu/hiking-trails/koko-crater-railway-trail

Diaz, J. (2022, September 20). *Everything you need to know before you visit Lanai.* HawaiianIslands.com. https://hawaiianislands.com/lanai/blog/everything-you-need-to-know-before-you-visit-lanai

Drillinger, M., & Seavey, L. (2023, April 13). *Fifteen best beaches on the Big Island of Hawaii, HI.* Planet Ware. https://www.planetware.com/hawaii/best-beaches-on-the-big-island-of-hawaii-hi-us-hi-153.htm

Duke Paoa Kahanamoku. (n.d.). Olympics. https://olympics.com/en/athletes/duke-paoa-kahanamoku

East Maui Taro Festival (25th Annual). (n.d.). The Hawaiian Islands. https://www.gohawaii.com/islands/events/east-maui-taro-festival-25th-annual

Events – Molokai Ka Hula Piko Hula celebration. (n.d.). Visit Molokai. https://visitmolokai.com/wp/events-molokai-ka-hula-piko-hula-celebration

Ewa Hotel Waikiki. (n.d.). Booking.com. https://www.booking.com/hotel/us/ewa-waikiki.en-gb.html

Experience Pacific harmony at the Honolulu Festival. (n.d.). Honolulu Festival. https://www.honolulufestival.com/en/festival

Fisherman's trail. (n.d.). AllTrails. https://www.alltrails.com/trail/hawaii/lanai/fishermans-trail--2

Freeborn, A. (2024, February 13). *Where to Stay in Molokai (2024 coolest areas!).* The Broke Backpacker. https://www.thebrokebackpacker.com/where-to-stay-in-molokai-usa

Fromholz, J. (2024, January 3). *What to pack for your Hawaii vacation (2024).* The Hawaii Vacation Guide. https://thehawaiivacationguide.com/what-to-pack-for-hawaii-vacation

Gallagher, K. (2020, August 4). *A guide to airports in Hawaii.* TripSavvy. https://www.tripsavvy.com/a-guide-to-airports-in-hawaii-5075270

Gellerman, E. (2023, October 2). *The ten best beaches on Kauai: Stunning spots you don't want to miss!* The Hawaii Vacation Guide. https://thehawaiivacationguide.com/best-beaches-kauai

Gellerman, E. (2024, January 19). *Where to stay on Kauai (it's a complicated decision).* The Hawaii Vacation Guide. https://thehawaiivacationguide.com/where-to-stay-on-kauai

Gilbertson, D. (2019, May 2). *First-timers' guide to Honolulu: 10 do's and don'ts.* USA TODAY. https://www.usatoday.com/story/travel/destinations/2019/05/02/honolulu-travel-tips-10-dos-and-donts-oahu-hawaii/3620429002

Halawa Valley Falls Cultural Hike. (n.d.). Halawa Valley Falls Cultural Hike. https://halawavalleymolokai.com/hikeoverview.html

Haleakalā National Park Maui. (n.d.). The Hawaiian Islands. https://www.gohawaii.com/islands/maui/regions/upcountry-maui/haleakala-national-park

Halema'uma'u Crater. (n.d.). NASA Earth Observatory. https://earthobservatory.nasa.gov/images/81781/halemaumau-crater

Hanapepe Town. (n.d.). Hawaii Guide. https://www.hawaii-guide.com/kauai/towns/hanapepe

Hawai'i Volcanoes National Park. (n.d.). The Hawaiian Islands. https://www.gohawaii.com/islands/hawaii-big-island/regions/kau/volcanoes-national-park

Hawaiian customs and traditions. (n.d.). The Hawaiian Islands. https://www.gohawaii.com/hawaiian-culture/traditions

Hawaiian values. (n.d.). Ainahau O Kaleponi Hawaiian Civic Club. http://www.aokhcc.org/about/hawaiian-values

Hawaii's Aloha festivals: A comprehensive guide. (n.d.). Real Hawaii Tours. https://www.realhawaiitours.com/guide/oahu/aloha-festivals

Helling, A. (2024, January 3). *Is Hawaii safe to visit in 2024 | safety concerns.* Travelers Worldwide. https://travellersworldwide.com/is-hawaii-safe

Henderson, C. (2023, November 24). *The best time to visit Hawaii for good weather, smaller crowds, deals, and more.* The Points Guy. https://thepointsguy.com/guide/best-time-to-visit-hawaii

Hilo Reeds Bay Hotel. (n.d.). Booking.com. https://www.booking.com/hotel/us/hilo-reeds-bay.en-gb.html

History and culture on Maui. (2023, August 29). Love Big Island. https://www.lovebigisland.com/maui/history-and-culture

History of Iolani Palace. (n.d.). Iolani Palace. https://www.iolanipalace.org/history

History of the festival. (n.d.). Merrie Monarch Festival. https://www.merriemonarch.com/history-of-the-festival

HNN Staff. (2022, June 11). *Celebrating its 150th anniversary, King Kamehameha's floral parade is back in Oahu.* Hawaii News Now. https://www.hawaiinewsnow.com/2022/06/11/celebrating-150th-anniversary-king-kamehameha-floral-parade-is-back-oahu

Hotel Moloka'i. Booking.com. https://www.booking.com/hotel/us/marc-molokai-shores.en-gb.html

How to buy tickets. (n.d.). Merrie Monarch Festival. https://www.merriemonarch.com/how-to-buy-tickets-2

How to go, Hā'ena. (n.d.). Go Hā'ena. https://gohaena.com/info-faqs

'Iao Valley State Park Maui. (n.d.). The Hawaiian Islands. https://www.gohawaii.com/islands/maui/regions/central-maui/iao-valley-state-park

Iao Valley State Monument. (n.d.). Hawaii State Parks. https://www.hawaiistateparks.org/parks/iao-valley-state-monument

Jamie. (2023, March 8). *Hiking the Pololū Valley Lookout trail.* Simply Wander. https://justsimplywander.com/pololu-valley-lookout-trail

Jessica. (n.d.-a). *Thirteen best beaches in Oahu (Don't miss these).* Bon Traveler. https://www.bontraveler.com/best-beaches-oahu-hawaii

Jessica. (n.d.-b). *The 11 best hotels in Oahu for families to stay.* Bon Traveler. https://www.bontraveler.com/best-hotels-oahu-for-families

Jessica. (n.d.-c). *The 20 best restaurants in Oahu.* Bon Traveler. https://www.bontraveler.com/best-restaurants-oahu

Kalalau Trail. (n.d.). Hawaii.gov. https://dlnr.hawaii.gov/dsp/hiking/kauai/kalalau-trail

Kamakou Preserve. (n.d.). The Hawaiian Islands. https://www.gohawaii.com/islands/molokai/regions/east-end/kamakou-preserve

Kamrowski, E. (2022, July 7). *The best time to visit Hawaii: A month-by-month guide*. Thrifty Traveler. https://thriftytraveler.com/guides/travel/best-time-to-visit-hawaii

Kapalua Coastal Trail. (2023, May 18). MauiHawaii.org. https://www.mauihawaii.org/sights/kapalua-coastal-trail

Kauaʻi Mokihana Festival. (n.d.). Mālie Foundation. https://www.maliefoundation.org/kaua-i-mokihana-festival

Kauai Palms Hotel. (n.d.). Booking.com. https://www.booking.com/hotel/us/kauai-palms.en-gb.html

Kauai's history. (n.d.). Kauai.com. https://www.kauai.com/kauai-history

Keahiakawelo. (n.d.). The Hawaiian Islands. https://www.gohawaii.com/islands/lanai/regions/north-lanai/Keahiakawelo

Kendrick, L. (2023, January 18). *Twenty-five famous landmarks in Hawaii to visit*. Destguides. https://www.destguides.com/united-states/hawaii/famous-hawaii-landmarks#uss_arizona_memorial

Kohala Village Inn. (n.d.). Tripadvisor. https://www.tripadvisor.ca/Hotel_Review-g60582-d113125-Reviews-Kohala_Village_Inn-Hawi_Island_of_Hawaii_Hawaii.html

Kōkeʻe State Park. (n.d.-a). The Hawaiian Islands. https://www.gohawaii.com/islands/kauai/regions/west-side/kokee-state-park

Kōkeʻe State Park. (n.d.-b). Hawaii.gov. https://dlnr.hawaii.gov/dsp/parks/kauai/kokee-state-park

Kokee State Park. (n.d.). Hawaiʻi State Parks. https://www.hawaiistateparks.org/parks/kokee-state-park

Koloiki Ridge Trail—Lanaʻi. (2018, September 1). The Hiking Hi. https://www.thehikinghi.com/single-post/2018/09/01/koloiki-ridge-trail-lanai

Kona Brewing Company. (n.d.). Big Island Guide. https://bigislandguide.com/kona-brewing-company

Kona Seaside Hotel. (n.d.). Agoda. https://www.agoda.com/kona-seaside-hotel/hotel/kailua-hi-us.html?cid=1844104&ds=WXTqKx6GU2CDfEKG

Kualoa Ranch tours. (n.d.). Hawaii Tours. https://www.hawaiitours.com/oahu/kualoa-ranch

Lānaʻi City. (n.d.). The Hawaiian Islands. https://www.gohawaii.com/islands/lanai/regions/central-lanai/lanai-city

Lanai Cat Sanctuary. (n.d.). The Hawaiian Islands. https://www.gohawaii.com/islands/lanai/lanai-cat-sanctuary/73360

Lanai City Bar & Grill. (n.d.). OpenTable. https://www.opentable.com/r/lanai-city-bar-and-grill-lanai-city

Law, L., & Seavey, L. (2023, December 27). *Twenty-one top attractions on the Big Island of Hawaii*. Planet Ware. https://www.planetware.com/tourist-attractions-/hawaii-big-island-of-hawaii-us-hi-h.htm

Lehnardt, K. (2019, September 4). *Fifty interesting facts about Hawaii*. FactRetriever. https://www.factretriever.com/hawaii-facts

Local Hawaiian comfort food. (n.d.). Hawaiian Style Café. https://hawaiianstylecafe.us/index.html

Love Big Island. (2023, July 22). *History and culture on Big Island*. https://www.lovebigisland.com/history-and-culture

Lyons-Makaimoku, L. (n.d.). *Beginner's guide to visiting the Hawaiian island of Molokai*. Matador Network. https://matadornetwork.com/read/beginners-guide-visiting-hawaiian-island-molokai

Makai Club Resort. (n.d.). Tripadvisor. https://www.tripadvisor.ca/Hotel_Review-g60626-d1488772-Reviews-Makai_Club_Resort-Princeville_Kauai_Hawaii.html

Marcie. (2022, August 30). *Ten things to know before planning a Big Island vacation*. Hawaii Travel Spot. https://hawaiitravelspot.com/planning-a-hawaii-big-island-vacation

Maui Ocean Breezes. (n.d.). Oyster. https://www.oyster.com/maui/hotels/maui-ocean-breezes

Maui public bus transit system. (n.d.). Maui County. https://www.mauicounty.gov/609/Maui-Bus-Public-Transit-System

Miner, M. (2014, October 9). *The 26th annual Eo e Emalani I Alakai Festival honors Hawaii's Queen Emma on Oct. 11 on Kauai*. Hawaii Magazine. https://www.hawaiimagazine.com/26th-annual-eo-e-emalani-i-alakai-festival-honors-hawaiis-queen-emma-oct-11-on-kauai

Moʻolelo (stories). (n.d.). National Park Service. https://www.nps.gov/havo/learn/historyculture/moolelo.htm

Molokai Island Retreat. (n.d.). The Hawaiian Islands. https://www.gohawaii.com/listing/molokai-island-retreat/114403

Molokai Shores. (n.d.). Booking.com. https://www.booking.com/hotel/us/molokai-shores-kaunakakai1.en-gb.html

Musker, J., & Clements, R. (Directors). (2016). *Moana* [Film]. Walt Disney Studio Motion Pictures.

Nakamura, K. Y. (2023, August 21). *Hawaii's long road to becoming America's 50th state*. HISTORY: A&E Television Networks. https://www.history.com/news/hawaii-50th-state-1959

Natural History Museum. (n.d.). *Why are coral reefs important?* National History Museum. https://www.nhm.ac.uk/discover/quick-questions/why-are-coral-reefs-important.html

O'Connell, M. (2012, July 20). *What Hawaii's colorful Obon festival season is all about*. Hawaii Magazine. https://www.hawaiimagazine.com/what-hawaiis-colorful-obon-festival-season-is-all-about

Old Kōloa Town. (n.d.). The Hawaiian Islands. https://www.gohawaii.com/islands/kauai/regions/south-shore/old-koloa-town

One Aloha Shave Ice. (n.d.). Yelp. https://www.yelp.ca/biz/one-aloha-shave-ice-kailua-kona

Our story. (n.d.-a). Umekes Restaurants. https://www.umekesrestaurants.com/about-us

Our story. (n.d.-b). Esters Fair Prospect. https://www.estersmaui.com/about-1

Our vision. (n.d.). Maui Ocean Center. https://mauioceancenter.com/our-story

OUTRIGGER Kauaʻi Beach Resort & Spa. (n.d.). Booking.com. https://www.booking.com/hotel/us/kauai-beach-resort.en-gb.html

Paniolo Hale. (n.d.). Booking.com. https://www.booking.com/hotel/us/paniolo-hale-k4-moe-maluhia-a-place-of-peaceful-dreams.en-gb.html

Patil, C. (n.d.). *Is Kauai safe to visit in 2023? (honest advice & tips)*. GoHitchhiking. https://www.gohitchhiking.com/is-kauai-safe/?expand_article=1

Payne, A. (Director). (2011). *The Descendants* [Film]. Searchlight Pictures.

Pearl Harbor. (2024, January 25). National Park Service. https://www.nps.gov/perl/index.htm

Pearl Harbor National Memorial. (n.d.). National Park Foundation. https://www.nationalparks.org/explore/parks/pearl-harbor-national-memorial

Prepare for an unforgettable journey to the heavenly Hana. (n.d.). Road to Hana. https://roadtohana.com

Prince Lot Hula Festival 2022: Celebrating 45 years. (2022, October 27). Bank of Hawaii. https://www.boh.com/blog/prince-lot-hula-festival-2022-celebrating-45-years

quickwhittravel. (2021, July 1). *Halawa Valley Cultural Hike, Molokai: Everything you need to know*. https://quickwhittravel.com/2019/05/15/halawa-valley-cultural-hike-molokai

Respect the culture: Dos and don'ts when you're in Hawaii. (n.d.). Royal Hawaiian Movers. https://www.royalhawaiianmovers.com/respect-the-culture-dos-and-donts-when-youre-in-hawaii

Romantic upcountry cottages. (n.d.). Kula Lodge & Restaurant. https://kulalodge.com/maui-accommodations

Royal Kona Resort. (n.d.). Booking.com. https://www.booking.com/hotel/us/royal-kona-resort.en-gb.html

Sands Of Kahana. (n.d.). Tripadvisor. https://www.tripadvisor.ca/Hotel_Review-g60634-d87322-Reviews-Sands_Of_Kahana-Lahaina_Maui_Hawaii.html

Sandy Beach, Molokai. (n.d.). To-Hawaii.com. https://www.to-hawaii.com/molokai/beaches/sandybeach.php

7th annual Olukai Hoʻolauleʻa festival in Maui. (n.d.). Freesurf Magazine. https://freesurfmagazine.com/7th-annual-olukai-hoolaulea-festival-in-maui

Shark's Bay – one of Lanai's most beautiful attractions. (n.d.). Only in Hawaii. https://onlyinhawaii.org/sharks-bay-lanai-hawaii

Shell Vacations Club Kona Coast Resort. (n.d.). Extra Holidays. https://www.shellhospitality.com/hotels/kona-coast-resort

Shute, M. (2022, August 2). The world's largest sea cliffs are right here in Hawaii, and you'll want to visit. Only in Your State. https://www.onlyinyourstate.com/hawaii/worlds-tallest-sea-cliffs-hi

Sixteen things not to do on Kauai. (n.d.). Kauai Vacation Rentals. https://www.parrishkauai.com/102999/what-not-to-do-on-kauai

Smith, C. (n.d.). Kapalua Coastal Trail Maui: What to know before you go. MauiHacks. https://mauihacks.com/kapalua-coastal-trail-maui-what-to-know-before-you-go

Smith, J. (2023a, November 23). Is it illegal to take sand from Hawaii beaches? Hawaii Star. https://www.hawaiistar.com/is-it-illegal-to-take-sand-from-hawaii

Smith, J. (2023b, December 20). How to get around In Hawaii: The complete guide - Hawaii Star. Hawaii Star. https://www.hawaiistar.com/how-to-get-around-in-hawaii/

Smith, J. (2023c, December 20). How to visit Hawaii ethically and responsibly. Hawaii Star. https://www.hawaiistar.com/how-to-visit-hawaii-ethically

Smith, W. (n.d.). Flag of Hawaii. In *Encyclopedia Britannica*. Retrieved February 17, 2024, from https://www.britannica.com/topic/flag-of-Hawaii

Snow, J. (2016, March 31). What is the Merrie Monarch Festival? A primer. Hawaii Magazine. https://www.hawaiimagazine.com/what-is-the-merrie-monarch-festival-a-primer

Space mission in Hawaii? Decades-old photos show astronauts training for Apollo moon landings. (2014, June 1). *National Post*. https://nationalpost.com/news/space-mission-in-hawaii-decades-old-photos-show-astronauts-training-for-apollo-moon-landings

Spielberg, S. (Director). (1993). *Jurassic Park* [Film]. Universal Studios.

Starr, M. (2022, March 1). *11 mind-blowing Molokai beaches you shouldn't miss*. Next Is... Hawaii. https://nextishawaii.com/molokai-beaches

Stay with us. (n.d.). Puʻu O Hoku Ranch. https://puuohoku.com/stay-with-us

Staying safe in Hawaii. (n.d.). The Hawaiian Islands. https://www.gohawaii.com/trip-planning/travel-smart/safety-tips

Story: Hawaiki. (n.d.). Te Ara. https://teara.govt.nz/en/hawaiki

Tassi, A. (n.d.). Best Hotels in Maui, HI. U.S. News. https://travel.usnews.com/Hotels/Maui_HI/

The Aloha Spirit of Hawaii. (n.d.). Hawaii Hideaways. https://www.hawaiihideaways.com/2014/01/the-aloha-spirit-of-hawaii

The beautifully haunting Lanai Shipwreck Beach. (n.d.). Travel to Paradise. https://traveltoparadise.com/lanai-shipwreck-beach

The Cliffs at Princeville. (n.d.). Booking.com. https://www.booking.com/hotel/us/the-cliffs-at-princeville.en-gb.html

The Editors of Encyclopaedia Britannica. (n.d.-a). Duke Kahanamoku. In *Encyclopedia Britannica*. Retrieved February 29, 2024, from https://www.britannica.com/biography/Duke-Kahanamoku

The Editors of Encyclopaedia Britannica. (n.d.-b). Hawaii. In *Encyclopedia Britannica*. Retrieved February 13, 2024, from https://www.britannica.com/place/Hawaii-island-Hawaii

The extraordinary surfing life of Duke Kahanamoku. (2019). Surfertoday. https://www.surfertoday.com/surfing/the-extraordinary-surfing-life-of-duke-kahanamoku

The Foundation for Global Sports Development. (2022, April 20). *Learn about the rich history of Hawaii*. PBS American Masters. https://www.pbs.org/wnet/americanmasters/learn-the-rich-history-of-hawaii/21599

The Hawaiian language. (n.d.). The Hawaiian Islands. https://www.gohawaii.com/hawaiian-culture/hawaiian-language-guide

The heritage and history of Kauai, Hawaii. (2023, March 7). Koloa Landing Resort. https://koloalandingresort.com/heritage-and-history-of-kauai

The Ka Molokai Makahiki Festival. (n.d.). HawaiiHideaways. https://hawaiihideaways.com/2014/01/the-ka-molokai-makahiki-festival

The magical island of Lanaʻi: 10 fun facts. (2018, November 7). Hawaii Ocean Project. https://hawaiioceanproject.com/the-magical-island-of-lanai-10-fun-facts

The rooms. (n.d.). Banyan Bed & Breakfast. https://www.bed-breakfast-maui.com/rooms

TheBus Fares. (n.d.). TheBus. https://www.thebus.org/Fare/TheBusFares.asp

31st annual Hawaiian slack key guitar festival "Kauaʻi style." (n.d.). Kauaʻi Festivals & Events. https://kauaifestivals.com/festival/31st-annual-hawaiian-slack-key-guitar-festival-kauai-style

38th Annual Kōloa Plantation Days Festival. (n.d.). The Hawaiian Islands. https://www.gohawaii.com/islands/events/38th-annual-k%C5%8Dloa-plantation-days-festival

Tiffany. (n.d.). Fifteen things not to do on Maui. Maui Accommodations Guide. https://www.mauiaccommodations.com/blog/15-things-not-maui

Top 10 Hawaii etiquette tips. (n.d.). Hawaii Aloha Travel. https://www.hawaii-aloha.com/podcast/top-10-hawaii-etiquette-tips

Top 10 tourist traps on Maui. (n.d.). Maui Kayak Adventures. https://mauikayakadventures.com/maui/tourist-traps-maui-10-things

Top 33 restaurants in Maui. (n.d.). Pride of Maui. https://www.prideofmaui.com/blog/dining/best-restaurants-maui

Tour the farm. (n.d.). Molokai Plumerias. https://molokaiplumerias.com/tours

Trattner, E. (2022, November 25). *Where to exchange currency while traveling*. Moneywise. https://moneywise.com/banking/banking-basics/how-to-exchange-currency

Treksplorer. (2022, February 14). *Ten beautiful beaches in Lanai are great for your Hawaii vacation.* https://www.treksplorer.com/best-beaches-lanai-hi-usa

Trevorrow, C. (Director). (2015). *Jurassic World* [Film]. Universal Pictures.

Trysta B. (2023, July 16). *Flying to Hawaii tips: Everything you need to know before your trip.* This Travel Dream. https://thistraveldream.com/flying-to-hawaii-tips

Trysta B. (2024, February 18). *The 18 best restaurants in Kauai right now.* This Travel Dream. https://thistraveldream.com/restaurants-kauai

Turner, C. (n.d.). *East Maui Taro Festival.* Road to Hana. https://roadtohana.com/east-maui-taro-festival.php

20 Hawai'i dishes you must try when traveling to the islands. (2023, May 2). Hawaii Magazine. https://www.hawaiimagazine.com/20-hawaii-dishes-you-must-try-when-traveling-to-the-islands

25th annual Lanai Pineapple Festival. (2017, June 30). Lanai 96763 Community. https://www.lanai96763.com/lanai-pineapple-festival-25

Ultimate guide to Obon festivals on Oahu in 2023. (n.d.). Locations. https://www.locationshawaii.com/news/events/ultimate-guide-to-obon-festivals-on-oahu

USS Arizona Memorial. (n.d.). Recreation.gov. https://www.recreation.gov/ticket/233338/ticket/16

Visit. (n.d.). The Byodo-in Temple. https://byodo-in.com/visit

Visit Anaehoomalu Bay Beach (A-Bay). (n.d.). Big Island Guide. https://bigislandguide.com/visit-anaehoomalu-bay-beach

Wai'anapanapa State Park. (n.d.). Hawaii State Parks. https://www.hawaiistateparks.org/parks/waianapanapa-state-park

Wai'ānapanapa State Park. (n.d.). Hawaii.gov. https://dlnr.hawaii.gov/dsp/parks/maui/waianapanapa-state-park

Wailua River State Park. (n.d.-a). Hawaii State Parks. https://www.hawaiistateparks.org/parks/wailua-river-state-park

Wailua River State Park. (n.d.-b). Hawaii.gov. https://dlnr.hawaii.gov/dsp/parks/kauai/wailua-river-state-park

Wanderlog staff. (2023, December 25). *Where to eat: the 16 best restaurants in Molokai.* Wanderlog. https://wanderlog.com/list/geoCategory/203480/where-to-eat-best-restaurants-in-molokai

Welcome. (n.d.). Pele's Other Garden. https://pelesothergarden.com/peles

Welcome to the 43rd Kapalua Wine & Food Festival. (n.d.). Kapalua Wine & Food Festival. https://kapaluawineandfoodfestival.com

Welcome to the Blue Ginger Café. (n.d.). Blue Ginger Café. https://www.bluegingercafelanai.com/index.html

What is reef-safe sunscreen? (n.d.). REI Co-Op. https://www.rei.com/learn/expert-advice/what-is-reef-safe-sunscreen.html

What it means to receive a lei. (n.d.). Skyline. https://www.skylinehawaii.com/blog/what-it-means-to-receive-a-lei

Where to eat: The ten best restaurants in Lanai. (n.d.). Hawaii Aloha Travel. https://wanderlog.com/list/geoCategory/203556/where-to-eat-best-restaurants-in-lanai

White Sands Hotel. (n.d.). Booking.com. https://www.booking.com/hotel/us/white-sands-honolulu.en-gb.html

Why does Hawaii celebrate Prince Kuhio Day? (n.d.). Hawaii Aloha Travel. https://www.hawaii-aloha.com/blog/why-does-hawaii-celebrate-prince-kuhio-day

Wianecki, S. (2023, February 21). *The 24 essential Maui restaurants.* Eater. https://www.eater.com/maps/best-restaurants-maui-hawaii

Ziemelis, J. (2018, April 27). *The annual Farm Festival at Hāmākua Harvest focuses on local food, products, and fun.* 365 Kona. https://www.365kona.com/hawaii-things-to-do/annual-farm-festival-hamakua-harvest-focuses-local-food-products-fun

Made in United States
Orlando, FL
09 September 2024